1066

Borgo Press Books by ROBERT SILVERBERG

1066
Challenge for a Throne: The Wars of the Roses
The Crusades

1066

by

Robert Silverberg

Writing as Franklin Hamilton

THE BORGO PRESS

MMX

Copyright © 1964, 1992 by Agberg, Ltd.
Introduction Copyright © 2010 by Agberg, Ltd.

All rights reserved.
No part of this book may be reproduced in any form without the expressed written consent of the publisher.

www.wildsidebooks.com

FIRST WILDSIDE EDITION

INTRODUCTION TO THE BORGO EDITION

From Franklin Hamilton to Robert Silverberg

Since 1955 I have primarily been a writer of science fiction, but in the early 1960s, when I was about six years along in what had been a very successful career, science fiction fell into hard times, with diminishing sales of books and magazines and a corresponding aversion to artistic risk by most of the editors who remained at work in the greatly shrunken field. (Things were so bad that many leading writers, editors, and readers took part in a famous symposium, *Who Killed Science Fiction*, that won an award at the next World Science Fiction Convention.)

Since it now had become impossible for me to continue earning a living as a full-time freelancing specialist in science fiction, I turned my writing activities elsewhere, and soon, drawing on my own interests in history and science, had established myself as a writer of non-fiction books for high school and college readers. The major publishers of such books—Holt, Putnam, Doubleday, Macmillan, and several more—welcomed them, and quickly I began winning awards for them and the attention of librarians, who readily bought each new one as it appeared. The first of the books was *Lost Cities and Vanished Civilizations* (1962), swiftly followed by several others on archaeological subjects—*Empires in the Dust, Man Before Adam, Sunken History, To the Rock of Darius,* etc. I wrote a book about Socrates. I wrote one about great medical men. I wrote one on Copernicus and Galileo. I wrote one about nuclear physics. I wrote one on the Indians of the Pueblos. It was a busy decade.

I wrote so many books on so many themes between 1961 and 1970, in fact, that it started to seem implausible that one writer could master such a wide range of subjects, although I have always been a good researcher and a very prolific writer. My publishers and I feared that book buyers would begin to question the quality of the work. So it became commercially desirable to conceal my prolificacy behind pseudonyms. When I did a couple of books about famous explorers, I used the byline "Walker Chapman." A biography of Winston Churchill was credited to "Edgar Black." And when, in 1964, I wrote a book about the Norman conquest of England, it was published (by the Dial Press, an important publisher of the day) under the name of "Franklin Hamilton."

There were three Franklin Hamilton books in all: *1066*, the Norman Conquest book, followed in 1965 by *The Crusades*, and in 1967 by *Challenge for a Throne*, which dealt with the Wars of the Roses. (A projected fourth book about the Byzantine Empire got caught in a publishing change and was abandoned.) They were good, solid books, beautifully illustrated by my friend Judith Ann Lawrence (the wife of science-fiction writer James

Blish), they were well received by reviewers, and they sold very well for many years.

Now, after several decades in publishing limbo, here they are back in print again—and, since I am no longer so prolific that my books jostle against each other for the attention of readers, I see no reason to continue to hide them behind a pseudonym, so I have placed my own name on them at last.

—Robert Silverberg
Oakland, California
August, 2010

CHAPTERS

I	A Throne at Stake	3
II	Anglo-Saxon England	15
III	Two Harolds and William	35
IV	The Gathering Clouds	63
V	Invasion!	87
VI	The Battle of Hastings	107
VII	The Aftermath of Conquest	135
VIII	Norman England	165
IX	"What If—?"	196

LIST OF ILLUSTRATIONS

Edward counsels Harold and a nobleman	8
Edward's death and the preparation for burial	11
Coronation of Harold	13
Britain and its invaders in 1065 (*map*)	19
Lineage of the four royal families	24-25
1033 (*map*)	28
Harold embarks for Normandy	53
William knights Harold	56
Harold swears upon his oath	58
Harold learns of the ominous "new star"	64
William confers with his counselors	75
Building and launching the fleet	82-83
The Norman fleet sails for England	102-103
The Normans burn Hastings	109
The beginning of the Battle of Hastings. October 14, 1066 (*map*)	119

List of Illustrations

The Normans ride to battle	122-123
The English defend the hill	127
Harold is killed	130
William's successive conquests in England (*map*)	151
Gytha flees with Harold's children to Ireland	153
William and his forces plunder Northumbria	159
William wounded at Mantes	189
The servants loot William's body	194

The majority of the illustrations are based directly on the well-known Bayeux tapestry. Woven in 1086, the tapestry portrays all the incidences of William's voyage to and conquest of England

None of the dialogue in this book is my invention. All spoken conversations are drawn from such near-contemporary sources as the Norse sagas, the Norman chroniclers such as William of Poitiers, and the various English chroniclers. In some cases I have adapted the words of these sources in the interests of simplicity and clarity, but I have not presumed to make up whole conversations out of my imagination.

Franklin Hamilton

"Ahem!" said the Mouse with an important air. "Are you all ready? This is the driest thing I know. Silence all round, if you please! 'William the Conqueror, whose cause was favored by the pope, was soon submitted to by the English, who wanted leaders, and had been of late much accustomed to usurpation and conquest. Edwin and Morcar, the earls of Mercia and Northumbria—'"

"Ugh!" said the Lory, with a shiver.

"I beg your pardon!" said the Mouse, frowning, but very politely. "Did you speak?"

"Not I!" said the Lory, hastily.

"I thought you did," said the Mouse. "I proceed. 'Edwin and Morcar, the earls of Mercia and Northumbria, declared for him; and even Stigand, the patriotic archbishop of Canterbury, found it advisable—'"

"Found *what*?" said the Duck.

"Found *it*," the Mouse replied rather crossly: "of course you know what 'it' means."

—Lewis Carroll,
Alice in Wonderland

1066

A THRONE AT STAKE

It was Christmas week of the year 1065, and a king lay dying in London.

He was Edward, whom men would later call Edward the Confessor, meaning Edward the Saint. He had ruled over England for twenty-three years, and he was neither the best nor worst of kings, and now his life was drawing to a close. He had been ill since October, and troubled by rebellions in the north of his kingdom. Since the first chill winds of winter had swept across the face of England, Edward had taken to his bed, had remained fast in his palace. He was a man past sixty, and his health had never been robust.

Tension gripped England as the old year waned. The king lay dying, and everyone knew it. But the king had no son to take his place on the throne. When Edward died, his dynasty died with him—a dynasty that traced its lineage back to King Alfred the Great, and through him back across four centuries to Cerdic, the first Saxon king of England.

Who would step forward to take the English throne?

In the circle round the dying king, men watched closely for some hint as to his wishes. Edward said nothing. His mind was far away. In the last years of his life his main joy had been the building of an abbey at Westminster, outside the western gate of London. Edward's abbey is not the Westminster Abbey of today, which was built some centuries later, but an earlier one that in its time was a grand and imposing sacred building. The old king had yearned to live to see it consecrated. But on the day of the ceremony, the twenty-eighth of December, 1065, he was too ill to attend the hallowing, and his queen had to take his place.

Now Edward's life ebbed with the dying year.

Three men hungered for his throne. In England, blond Harold, Earl of Wessex, the brother-in-law of the king, waited none too patiently for a chance to place Edward's crown upon his own head. Across the English Channel in Normandy dwelled dark, brooding Duke William, who felt that he had a right to rule England after Edward. And far off in stormy Norway lived yet another claimant, a giant of a man, mighty Harold Hardrada, Norway's monarch and the last of the great Viking princes. These three all felt they had honest title to the English crown.

Nor were they alone. Sweyn Estrithson, King of Denmark, also thought he had a claim, but few took him seriously. And there was even a rightful claimant of royal blood: Edgar the Atheling, Edgar the Prince, son of King Edward's nephew. Edgar, though, was only a boy in his teens. These were troubled times in Europe, no moment to place a boy on the throne. The nobles of England had already quietly agreed that Edgar could not be king.

Of the mounting tension the dying Edward took no notice. He had been king since 1042, when he succeeded a usurping Dane, Harthacnut (or Hardacanute), as England's king. Edward had been about thirty-seven then, and had spent most of his life, up to that time, overseas, an exile in his mother's country of Normandy while Danes ruled England. Coming to the throne when Harthacnut died, Edward was practically a stranger to England. The language he spoke best was Norman French; he observed Norman customs, and his closest friends were Normans—such as his cousin William, Duke of Normandy.

Edward had not particularly wanted to be King of England. He was a quiet, retiring man who preferred to spend his time at prayer, or else at the hunt. But royal blood flowed in his veins, and the nobles of England had brought him out of Normandy to be their king when the hated Harthacnut, still a young man, "fell to the earth in a horrid convulsion as he stood at his drink, and died on the spot," as the chronicler tells us.

Edward was a strange man to behold. His hair and beard early turned white, and his face was oddly pinkish. So long and thin and pale were his hands that they looked almost transparent. He cared little for drinking and carousing, and not at all for the love of fair women. When he came to the throne, he brought with him friends from Normandy and put them into power around him. The most important of these was Robert, a Norman priest, whom Edward first made Bishop of London and then named as Archbishop of Canterbury, head of the Church in England.

The powerful nobles of England resented the presence of these foreigners, who, they said, "promoted injustice, gave unjust judgments, and counseled folly." Most outspoken of all was Godwin, Earl of Wessex, who finally forced Edward to send his Normans back to Normandy. Archbishop Robert fled, and an Englishman named Stigand replaced him in the cathedral at Canterbury. Edward took Godwin's daughter Edith as his queen, and Godwin and two of his sons, Harold and Tostig, came to wield great power in England.

An old chronicle declares,

> And so, with the kingdom made safe on all sides by these princes [Earl Harold and his brother], the most kindly King Edward passed his life in security and peace, and spent much of his time in the glades and woods in the pleasures of hunting. After divine service, which he gladly and devoutly attended every day, he took much pleasure in hawks and birds of that kind which they brought before him, and was really delighted by the baying and scrambling of the hounds.

He was an odd mixture of saintliness and bloodthirstiness, this Edward the Confessor. After praying for hours on end, he would go into the forests and butcher wild animals with savage ferocity. Whenever trouble arose anywhere in the kingdom, his way of dealing with it was to send troops to harry and sack the towns of the offenders.

Though he was not a dynamic man, Edward sometimes was able to assert himself vigorously. He did so in 1051, when he had ruled for nine years under the influence of Godwin of Wessex. A quarrel arose between Edward and Godwin. Edward took advantage of the situation to force Godwin and his sons into exile. For the first time since he had come to the throne, Edward was free of the domineering Wessex earl.

The king made good use of his new freedom. A new horde of Normans crossed the Channel to take up residence at Edward's court—the very thing Godwin and his son Harold had opposed. And a very curious visit took place. In those days it was almost unheard of for one ruler to journey to visit another. Yet out of Normandy came the twenty-five-year-old Duke William, Edward's cousin, to visit England! The chronicles of England say simply, "William Earl came from beyond sea with mickle company of Frenchmen, and the King received him, and as many of his comrades as to him seemed good, and let him go again."

What happened during this unusual visit? What did the young Duke of Normandy and the aging King of England say to one another?

Their conversation will always remain history's secret. But Duke William ever after claimed that at their meeting the childless Edward had promised him, "You shall have the throne of England after me."

Soon after—in the spring of 1052—Godwin and Harold returned from exile. They had gathered a great army, and though the king too had soldiers, "it was loathful to almost all of them to fight against men of their own race." Weakening, Edward agreed to make peace with his stormy earl. Godwin and Harold returned to power. It was at this time that Archbishop Robert and the rest of Edward's Normans were forced to flee from England. From that time on, no more was said of Duke William's claim to Edward's throne.

Godwin died suddenly in April, 1053, and his son Harold became the leading figure in England. For the next dozen years, Harold, like his father, served as "under-king," and it was he who really ruled England while Edward gave himself up to the pleasures of the hunt and to his religious

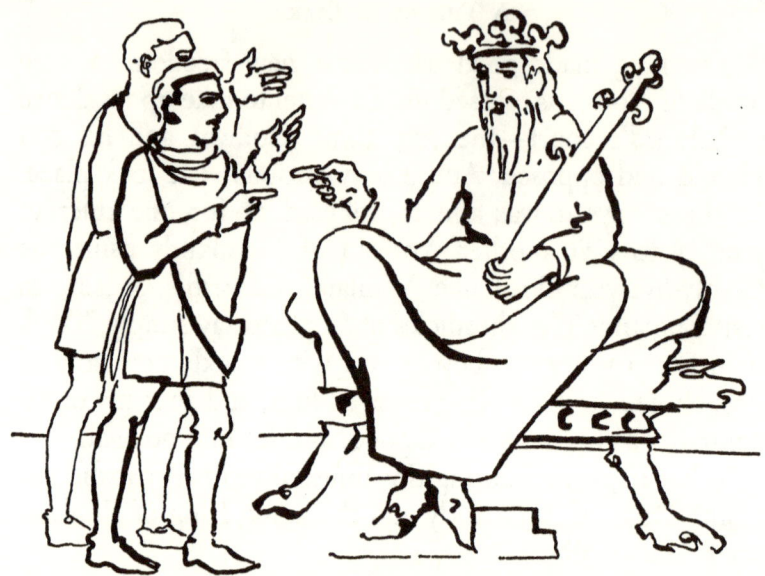

Edward counsels Harold and a nobleman

piety. The arrangement was openly known, and gradually it came to seem as though Harold would almost certainly inherit England's throne when Edward died. But, as we will see, a strange twist of fate gave Duke William new reason to claim the throne.

As Edward grew older and more feeble, the matter of his successor came to have gigantic importance in Europe. Today there can never be any doubt about the succession to the English throne. Carefully planned laws designate the heir, and the succession is known to thirty or forty places. When an English king dies, the throne goes to his eldest son—or to his eldest daughter if there are no sons. If there are no children at all, the crown passes to the eldest brother of the king. Even if no brothers or sisters of the king are alive, the laws of succession still point to the next in line.

It was all quite different nine centuries ago. In some

countries succession was by inheritance, the oldest male child of the king taking the throne. In other lands succession was by election, with a council of nobles and bishops choosing the new monarch. Elsewhere usurpation and conquest were the usual events; the throne was seized by right of might.

In England of the eleventh century all three systems were in use. Inheritance mattered; the new king was supposed to be "of royal blood," preferably a descendant of the great Saxon kings of the past, Alfred and his ancestor Cerdic. Election also played a part; the *witenagemot*, or *witan*, a council of English nobles and church leaders, supposedly had the right to choose the king from among the leading members of the royal family. And, finally, an element of conquest had entered the picture, since only three kings in the past hundred and fifty years had reached the throne without having to fight for it.

The situation was confusing. There were no agreed rules of the game. Who would inherit?

By the right of descent, the throne should go to young Edgar the Atheling. He was the son of Edward the Atheling, long an exile in Hungary, who had died in 1054. And Edward the Atheling had been the son of Edmund Ironside, who was King of England for a few months in 1016. Edmund, in turn, was the half-brother of King Edward the Confessor. They both were sons of King Ethelred "the Unready," who was driven from his throne by Danish invaders.

Grandson of one king, great-grandson of another, grand-nephew of a third, Edgar the Atheling certainly had full title to the throne. But he was deemed too young to rule and was cast aside.

The other claimants to Edward's crown were not of royal Saxon descent. Harold was the king's brother-in-law, true, but that scarcely made him of royal blood. His father Godwin, though a Saxon, was part Danish, and not descended from Alfred the Great at all. As for Duke William of Normandy, his great-aunt Emma was the mother of Edward the Confessor, and his wife was a descendant of the Saxon king Cerdic—but neither of those facts made *him* a member of the Saxon royal family either! And Sweyn of Denmark and Harold Hardrada of Norway, the other two contenders, certainly had no Saxon blood. We will look at the nature of their claims later on.

Since none of the real contenders could claim the throne by right of blood, succession became a matter of "election"—meaning, actually, force. He who could command the strongest following could make himself King of England.

Would it be Harold of Wessex, or William of Normandy? Harold Hardrada of Norway? Sweyn Estrithson of Denmark?

The answer seemed clear as 1065 yielded to the new year. William, Sweyn, and Harold Hardrada were all far away. Harold of Wessex, son of Godwin, was at hand, waiting at the king's bedside, as was fitting for the realm's first earl. Edward clung to life in January's first days. On his deathbed—so says a biography of him written soon after—he prophesied dire evils that would come upon England. He saw the approaching ruin of England, which he said was "doomed by God to destruction because of the wickedness of its rulers."

Four people watched the old king's death agonies: Edith the Queen, her brother Earl Harold, Archbishop Stigand of Canterbury, and Robert FitzWymarc, the King's chamberlain. As Edward continued to mutter darkly of the visions

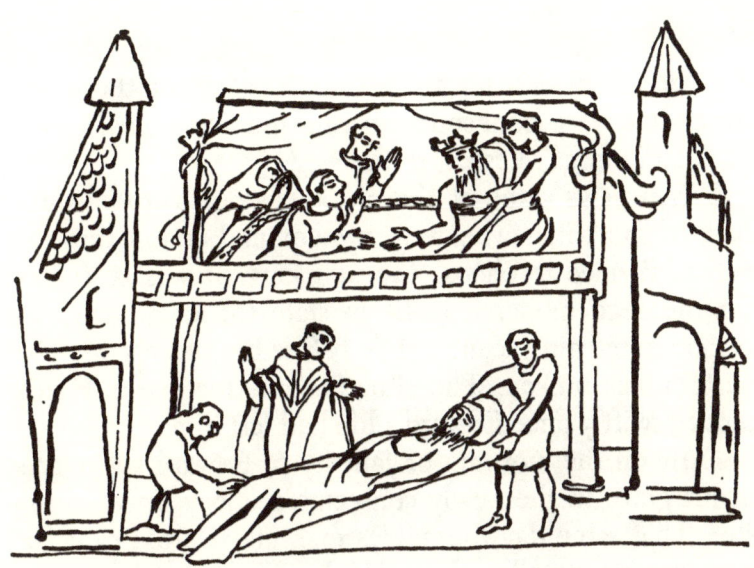

Edward's death and the preparation for burial

of doom that he saw, Archbishop Stigand is said to have turned to Harold and whispered, "The king is worn out by age and infirmity. He babbles of he knows not what."

On January 5 of the fateful year 1066, Edward's end approached. A Norse saga written not long afterward relates that "when the king was about to die Harold and a few others were with him. Harold bent down over him and said, 'I call you to witness that the king just now gave me the kingship, and the rule over all England.' Then the dead king was carried away from his bed."

But Edward did not have the right to proclaim Harold as his successor. That could only be done by the witan, the great council—which, of course, would heed the late king's dying wish.

Edward had been long in dying, and many of England's nobility had gathered in London to await the change of reigns. Few nobles had come from Northumbria and Mercia, though, which lay to the north. Most of those who were there were from southern England and from Harold's own earldom of Wessex, to the west.

When news came of the old king's death, those members of the witan who were present in London came together at once to choose the new king. It was customary for the dead monarch to lie in state for a few days, the throne to remain vacant awhile before the succession. That custom was broken. The situation was too tense. Harold moved swiftly once Edward's life had left him.

Early on the morning of January 6, Edward was placed in his grave in the newly consecrated abbey of Westminster. That same day the nobles met, and Harold came before them to state his claim. With a speed that leads us to think it was all arranged and rehearsed beforehand, Earl Harold of Wessex, then about forty years old and at the height of his strength, was elected King of England.

Before night had fallen, on that busy sixth of January, 1066, Harold had been anointed and crowned, and had mounted the throne, and into his hands had been placed the scepter and the battle-ax that symbolized his new power. The task of anointing the new king rightfully belonged to the Archbishop of Canterbury. But Stigand had been denounced by the pope because he held not only the Canterbury post but that of Bishop of Winchester as well, in defiance of Church law. Harold was unwilling to begin his reign by defying the pope. So the controverisal Stigand stepped aside, and the rites of coronation were performed by Eldred, Archbishop of York.

Harold was destined to have neither a long nor a glorious reign. "It was prophesied," an ancient chronicler writes, "that his rule would be a time of little ease."

Coronation of Harold

On the sixth of January, at least, Harold occupied the English throne, as he would for nine months thereafter. But even on that day when, as the chronicle says, "he succeeded to the kingdom as the King granted it to him and as he was chosen thereto," opposition began to rise.

First of the enemies was Harold's own brother Tostig. While the nobles of England did homage to King Harold, Tostig stood apart, airing his displeasure. "I want," he said, "the chiefs of the land to choose the man whom they think most fit to be king." Harold heard his brother's words and retorted that the chiefs of the land had chosen him, and that he would not yield the kingship to any man, "For he had been placed on the king's high seat in Edward's place, and had been anointed and consecrated."

On that very day, though, messengers were speeding abroad—to fierce William of Normandy, to towering Harold Hardrada of Norway. They brought to those bold warriors the news that Harold of Essex, moving forcefully and hastily, had grasped Edward's crown before Edward's body was hardly cold.

Harold must have known that day, as he listened to the shouts of the men who had just named him king, that before long he would have to fight to defend the prize he had seized. War was in the air—dark, terrible war that would take the lives of two kings and thousands of knights, war that would change the pattern of the world's history.

ANGLO-SAXON ENGLAND

WHAT KIND OF LAND WAS THIS ENGLAND of the Anglo-Saxons? What sort of prize was it over which dukes and kings would contend in the somber year 1066?

It was a rich land of rolling hills and fertile fields, of thriving towns and busy cities. Imposing churches and cathedrals told of the strength of religion in the England of Edward the Confessor. Skilled monks produced masterpieces of illuminated manuscripts, wrote historical chronicles and works of poetry. The work of English goldsmiths was famous throughout Europe. The silver pennies of England were the handsomest coins then being struck, and English currency was sounder than any other. England had a long historical tradition; it had an elaborate system of justice, an extensive body of written and unwritten law. Isolated from Europe by water, England had developed a vigorous and sophisticated civilization.

But there were grave weaknesses in England's political structure in the time of Edward the Confessor. Two centuries before, Alfred the Great had rallied England at a time when it tottered under the attacks of Danish raiders, had welded the separate and warring kingdoms of England together and made them strong in union. Alfred's son, Edward the Elder, and Edward's sons, Athelstan, Edmund, and Edred, had ruled wisely and well. Edgar, son of Edmund, enjoyed a long and successful reign also. But soon after him the royal house of England had come upon hard times. A series of short-lived, weak kings had occupied the throne, and finally the Danes returned, driving a pitiful great-great-grandson of Alfred the Great into exile and actually placing themselves on the throne.

The death of Harthacnut had ended Danish rule and given the crown back to the dynasty of Alfred. Edward the Confessor, though, was as weak a king as his father Ethelred had been, and in Edward's day England's strength crumbled. There had never been any strong feeling of English national unity. A man of Edward's day was not likely to say, "I am an Englishman!" Rather would he declare, "I am a man of Wessex," or, "I am a Mercian," or, "I am of Northumbria," declaring his allegiance to his local district rather than to the nation as a whole.

It was out of the same feeling, or lack of feeling, that Englishmen of Edward's day had little interest in fighting to defend their country. It does not seem to have mattered to most of the people whether a descendant of Alfred ruled them, or a Dane, or a Norwegian, or a Norman Frenchman.

The King of England was anything but a powerful absolute monarch. Over the years earls and nobles had carved out little domains for themselves within England, and their word was heeded more often than the king's. In his history of England, *The Birth of Britain*, Sir Winston Churchill has written:

> Though England was still the only state in Europe with a royal treasury to which sheriffs all over the country had to account, royal control over the sheriffs had grown lax. The King lived largely upon his private estates and governed as best he could through his household. The remaining powers of the monarchy were in practice severely restricted by a little group of Anglo-Danish notables. The main basis of support for the English kings had always been this select Council, never more than sixty, who in a vague manner regarded themselves as the representatives of the whole country. . . . But at this time this assembly of 'wise men' in no way embodied the life of the nation. It weakened the royal executive without adding any strength of its own. Its character and quality suffered in the general decay. It tended to fall into the hands of the great families. As the central power declined a host of local chieftains disputed and intrigued in every county, pursuing private and family aims and knowing no interest but their own. Feuds and disturbances were rife.

England's morale had been rocked and shattered by the Danish invasions of 1009–12, which culminated in the presence of a Danish dynasty on the English throne in 1013. Even after Edward the Confessor returned from exile to rule, an atmosphere of defeat and discouragement clouded England's life. Three great earls—Godwin of Wessex, Leofric of Mercia, and Siward of Northumbria—had come to exercise as much power in their districts as Edward himself. Wales, far to the west, was in the hands of local chieftains, rebellious enemies of Edward. Scotland, too, was independent—ruled in Edward's day by a treacherous usurper, Macbeth by name, given by Shakespeare an immortality he could not have imagined.

A weak and divided land, yet a rich and prospering one! Small wonder that it seemed a tempting prize for foreign invaders. We can readily see why Harold Hardrada of the frosty northlands cast covetous eyes at "England's green and pleasant land." And William of Normandy, a scant eighty miles from England's shores, ruling a dukedom only 190 miles from northeast to southwest, a dukedom smaller than the English earldom of Wessex alone, thirsted to add his wealthy neighbor to his domain.

Ironically the Anglo-Saxons themselves held England by right of conquest. Long before they first set foot on that island, it had been the Roman province of Brittania, inhabited by a mixed population of native dwellers—a Celtic people called the Britons—and by Roman colonists. The decline of Rome had left Brittania, or Britain, isolated and defenseless at Europe's western end. The Britons, who were Christians and who had attained a high civilization, were invaded, from about A.D. 450 on, by barbaric heathens who came from the northern mainland of the Continent.

There were three separate, but related and similar, groups of invaders: the Angles, who occupied the midlands and the north; the Saxons, who took possession of western and central zones; and the Jutes, who claimed what is now Kent, the southeastern part of England. The early history of the Anglo-Saxon invasion of Britain is shrouded in uncertainty. Out of the mist shines the legend of Arthur, last

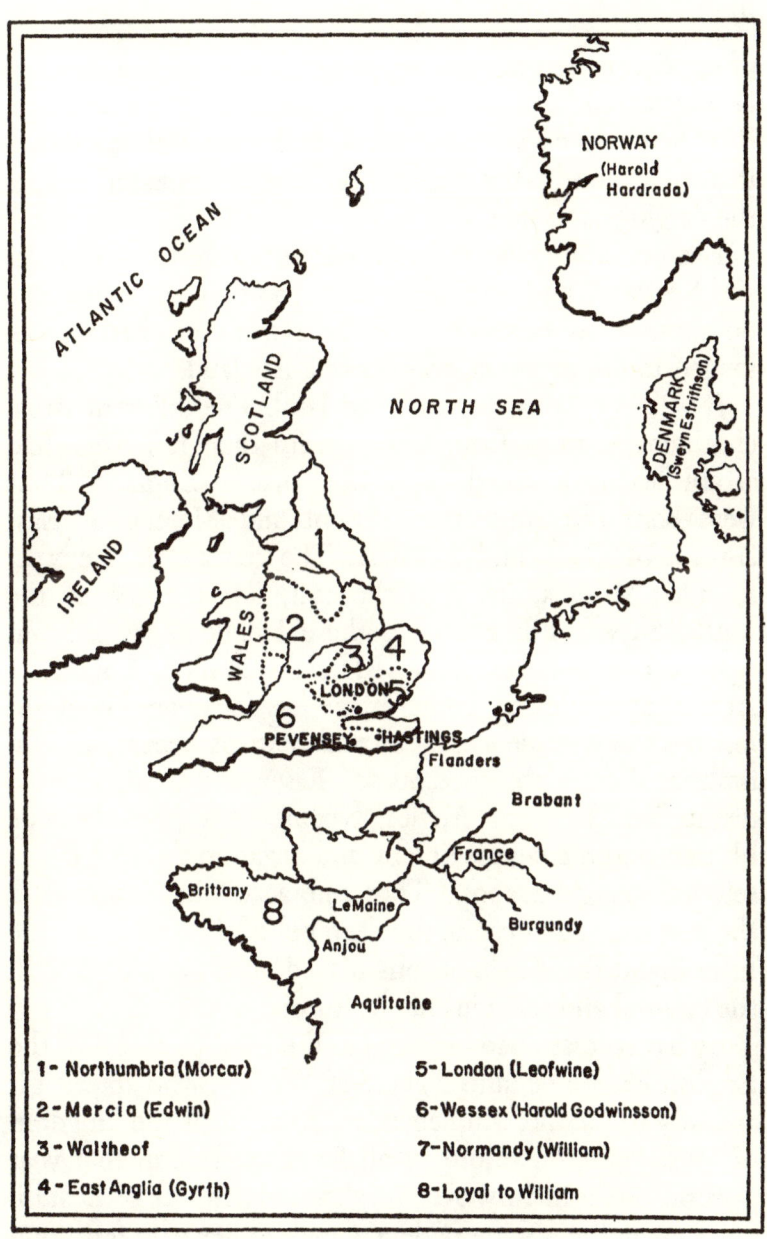

Britain and its invaders in 1065

of the Briton heroes, who supposedly defeated the invaders at a great battle and temporarily checked their advance. But there was no stopping them, and after Arthur's day—if ever he lived—the Britons stubbornly retreated before the Anglo-Saxon tide.

Eventually they were driven out completely, into Wales and Scotland, and after about A.D. 700 they could manage no more than occasional border skirmishes. Britain belonged to the invaders, and became England.

It was not, however, a unified land. The different tribal chieftains, coming from Europe with their followers, had established little kingdoms of their own in England. Thus were born the kingdoms of Kent and Mercia, of East Anglia, of Deira and Bernicia. The Saxons of the west founded Wessex, those of the east, Essex, those of the south, Sussex. For centuries these kingdoms waged war against one another. Now Mercia prevailed, now East Anglia, now Wessex. Some of the less fortunate kingdoms lost their independence. Deira and Bernicia became Northumbria; Wessex absorbed Sussex, Essex, and Kent. The old distinctions between Angles, Saxons, and Jutes became blurred, and the people of England began to think of themselves as "Anglo-Saxons." They embraced Christianity after the year 600, and despite the deep political divisions on the little island the Anglo-Saxons played an important role in the cultural and religious life of Europe.

By 835 Wessex had emerged as the most powerful of the English kingdoms, and Egbert of Wessex, who traced his ancestry to Cerdic, semilegendary founder of the kingdom of Wessex, was overlord of all England. But in that year a storm broke in fury over England: down out of Scandinavia came the Viking raiders, dread pirates who fell upon wealthy England like hungry wolves.

The Vikings came as pirates, but they ended as settlers. All during the rest of the ninth century they first conquered, then colonized England, devouring it from the east and from the north. By 871, when Alfred came to the English throne, only Wessex still remained free of Danish rule. The Danes had put an end to the royal dynasties of the other kingdoms, and they came close to swallowing up Wessex as well.

Alfred prevailed. He drove the Danes back, came to terms with them, restored peace. Much of England remained in Danish hands, but there was no further warfare. Alfred's great-grandson Edgar, who ruled from 959 to 975, made a formal treaty with the Danes of eastern England. They agreed to swear loyalty to the King of England, who was of the royal dynasty of Wessex. In return, Edgar agreed to grant the Danes a large measure of self-government, permitting them to abide by their own laws and customs, under his authority. Because the Danish part of England had its own laws, the district soon became known as the Danelaw. The once fierce pirates became farmers and villagers, and so diligently did they labor that the Danelaw contained the three most prosperous counties of Anglo-Saxon England: Suffolk, Norfolk, and Lincolnshire.

England thus came to be the home of two groups. There were the Anglo-Saxons, and there were the Danes. Relations between the two peoples were friendly, and intermarriage slowly began to unite them in language, law, and customs.

Toward the end of the tenth century there was again a stirring in Denmark. For a hundred years there had been no Danish invasions of England, but now the Vikings took to the sea again. Denmark had been weakened by internal strife during the century of peace. Now, under the fierce

King Sweyn, the Danes set out to finish the job of conquering England.

The peaceful reign of Edgar had ended in 975, and he had left two youngs sons by different mothers. The elder came to the throne as Edward II, but after a rule of three years he was treacherously slain by partisans of his young half-brother. Then, his rule stained by the martyrdom of Edward II, there became king a child of ten, Ethelred. With Danes threatening to invade, it was no time to make a boy king.

Ethelred has won an unhappy place in history. Weak and self-indulgent, thoughtless and vain, he brought defeat upon England and disgrace upon himself. He was rewarded with the nickname, Ethelred *"Unrede,"* which meant Ethelred the Ill-Advised, Ethelred the Unwise. Later the original Saxon meaning of *unrede* was forgotten, and today he is usually known by the punning but inaccurate name of Ethelred the Unready.

He was still a boy when the Danish raids began. Marauders from Denmark massacred the inhabitants of village after village, then sent word that they were willing to be bought off. "We will with gold set up a truce," they declared. King Ethelred preferred to bribe them rather than to fight. He laid heavy taxes, known as Danegeld, upon his people. In 991 he paid 10,000 pounds of silver to have peace; in 994, 16,000 pounds more; in 1002, another 24,000 pounds.

The Danes grew ever greedier and increased their demands. Suddenly, in 1002, Ethelred found his missing courage and hatched a dastardly scheme. He ordered the massacre of every Dane then living in the south of England, even those who were loyal to his rule. The slaughter was carried out, and one of the victims was Gunnhild, sister of King Sweyn of Denmark.

Revenge was swift. For two years Sweyn sacked and plundered England. Then he withdrew, after the pitiful Ethelred once again bribed him with a vast quantity of silver.

In 1009 England belatedly started to build a navy to fend off Viking attacks. "But," the chronicle observes, "we had not the good fortune nor the worthiness that the ship-force could be of any use to this land." Sweyn swooped down again and again. Thousands of pounds more of silver went into the Danish treasury. The Archbishop of Canterbury himself was slain by Viking seamen. In 1013 Sweyn, accompanied by his son Cnut (or Canute), landed in northern England and began to march through the Danelaw toward London.

Forced to choose between foolish King Ethelred and fierce King Sweyn, the Danes of northern England shifted their allegiance to their kinsman Sweyn. As he marched south town after town hailed him as king, even beyond the Danelaw. Ethelred sent his wife Emma into Normandy for safety, and then, at the end of 1013, followed her into ignominious exile. Sweyn of Denmark was hailed as England's king.

Ethelred's first wife had died in her youth, after bearing several sons, including Edmund, heir to the English throne. For his second wife Ethelred had taken Emma, daughter of Duke Richard I of Normandy. Emma had given Ethelred two sons, Alfred and Edward. (The same Edward who later was known as Edward the Confessor.)

Ethelred huddled for refuge at Rouen, where Emma's brother, Duke Richard II of Normandy, had his court.

Lineage of the four royal families

Only a few months later, on February 3, 1014, Sweyn died. His empire was divided. His elder son Harold succeeded him on the throne of Denmark. His younger son Cnut was recognized by the Danelaw of England as ruler. The earls of southern England, however, refused to bow to Cnut. They sent for exiled Ethelred, "declaring that no lord was dearer to them than their natural lord, if he would but rule them better than he had done before." But Ethelred's eldest son, Edmund, acted independently of his father, attacking the Danes while Ethelred feebly sought peace with them. This led to near civil war between father and son.

Ethelred occupied the throne of part of England for two years. He died in 1016, and Edmund, nicknamed Ironside for his valor, became king. In his brief but brilliant career Edmund Ironside won battle after battle from Cnut's Danes, and after six months the two young leaders agreed upon a truce. England would be divided. Cnut would rule in the north, Edmund in the south.

In November of 1016 Edmund suddenly died, only twenty-two years old. Since Edmund's son and heir, Edward the Atheling, was only a baby, Cnut had a clear path to the throne of all England. The witan met in a spirit of despair, and, according to the chronicle, "The whole land chose Cnut as king, and of its own accord submitted itself to the man against whom it had previously made such a strenuous resistance."

Edward the Atheling, son of Edmund Ironside, was packed off to distant Hungary as an infant exile. But there were also some other sons of Ethelred alive. Eadwig, a full brother of Edmund Ironside, tried to rebel against Cnut, but was hunted down and slain. The two children of Ethelred and Emma, thirteen-year-old Alfred and twelve-year-old Edward, were sent to be raised at the court of the Duke of Normandy.

Emma, Ethelred's Norman widow, now did a startling thing. She married Cnut, whose father had driven Ethelred from his throne! She was fifteen years older than Cnut, and the Dane was already married to boot. In the casual way of his times he declared that his first marriage had been only "temporary" and dissolved it, taking Emma as his wife. The widow of one king of England, Emma became the wife of another—and the mother of two more.

Emma and Cnut had a son, Harthacnut, who was named as his father's heir. In a strange and unnatural way Emma turned against her two sons by Ethelred, Alfred and Edward. She disowned them completely.

Cnut unexpectedly proved to be a wise and just king, and, though a foreigner, was greatly loved by his English subjects. On the death of his brother Harold in that same year of 1016, Cnut became King of Denmark, and in 1028 he conquered Norway as well, something his father Sweyn had dreamed of without achieving. In 1035, when still a young man, Cnut died suddenly—and, as so often happens, his empire collapsed.

Cnut had hoped that England and Denmark would remain united and would be ruled by his son Harthacnut. His son Sweyn, by his first marriage, was to be King of Norway. But when Cnut died, Harthacnut was in Denmark, and before he could return to England to claim his inheritance, a usurper had seized it.

He was a young man named Harold, nicknamed Harold Harefoot for his swiftness. A son of Cnut by the first marraige, Harold Harefoot was not provided for by his father, and so helped himself. It is a sign of England's weakness

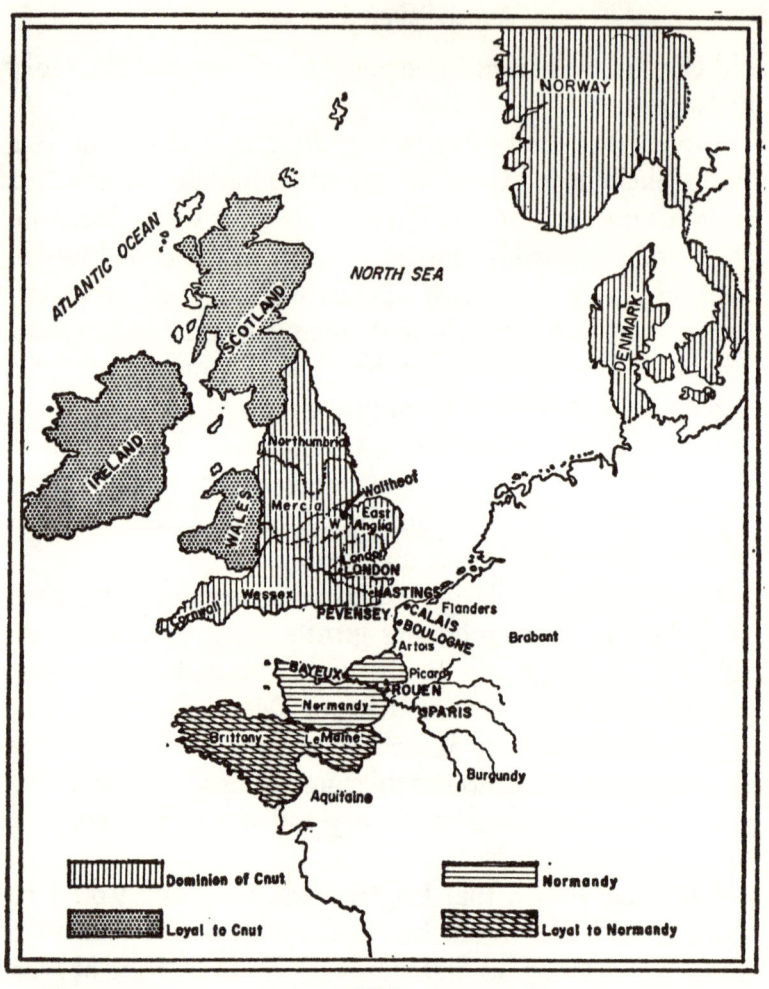

1033

at this time that an ambitious boy of twenty could grab the throne so easily.

Harold Harefoot ruled in England, and his half-brother Harthacnut in Denmark. The third brother, Sweyn, was driven out of Norway and Magnus, of the old Norwegian royal line, took his place. Harthacnut, after failing at an attempt to seize Norway himself after Sweyn's death, laid plans for regaining England from the usurper Harefoot.

While the sons of Cnut were quarreling, an exiled English prince began to have thoughts of dispossessing both of them. This was Alfred, Ethelred's son by Emma—now thirty-two years old. In 1035, while Cnut still lived, Alfred had actually persuaded his cousin Robert, now Duke of Normandy, to launch an invasion against England on his behalf. Robert assembled a fleet, but it was broken up in a storm, and this first Norman invasion of England came to nothing.

A year later Alfred tried again. He landed in Kent with six hundred Norman soldiers. He claimed that he was simply coming to visit his mother Emma. One does not usually pay a visit accompanied by six hundred soldiers, and Alfred's statement fooled nobody. It was quite clear that Ethelred's son had come with the intent of pushing Harold Harefoot from the throne.

He was met by Earl Godwin of Wessex. Godwin had emerged somewhat mysteriously onto the English scene about 1018 as a favorite of Cnut's. A man of great ability and even greater ambition, Godwin rapidly increased his influence in England, not always in a scrupulous way.

Godwin believed that Harthacnut was the rightful ruler of England, and not Harold Harefoot or Alfred. Meeting Alfred at Kent, Godwin feasted him in a friendly way and arranged lodgings for him and his men. At midnight a group of King Harold Harefoot's men appeared, seized Alfred, and slaughtered his sleeping soldiers. Alfred was imprisoned and blinded with such ferocity that he died soon afterward. Godwin always insisted thereafter that he had had no part in the brutal act—but his name is tainted with the suspicion that he deliberately handed Alfred over to Harold Harefoot's men.

The slaying of Alfred removed one claimant to the English throne. In 1040 Harold Harefoot himself died, young and childless. Harthacnut of Denmark wasted no time in stating his claim to the English throne, and three months after Harold's death the witan acclaimed Harthacnut as king.

His first royal act was to order Harold Harefoot's body to be taken from the grave and cast into the Thames. The rest of his reign was equally vicious. He was only twenty-five when death took him suddenly, in 1042. The last of Cnut's sons was dead. Before his death—in fact, before his accession to the English throne—Harthacnut had concluded a treaty with Magnus of Norway which is of some importance to our story. The Dane and the Norwegian agreed that if either should die without an heir, his kingdom should pass to the other.

By this treaty Magnus of Norway considered that he had the right to the English throne. But events moved too fast for him. By the time the Norwegian could press his claim, England already had a new king: Edward, son of Ethelred.

There were other claimants. There was Edward the Exile, son of Edmund Ironside, now twenty-six and still dwelling in distant Hungary. But he had few friends in England, and no one who would back his claim. There were also three sons of Cnut's sister Estrith—Sweyn, Osbeorn, and Beorn.

But Edward the Confessor, that mild-mannered and austerely religious man, happened to be in England when Harthacnut died. He had been invited to England by his half-brother Harthacnut, and soon after his departure from

Normandy found himself being hailed as England's king. The only one who spoke out against Edward was his own mother, Emma. Still nursing her hatred of her sons by Ethelred and her fondness for Scandinavian princes, Emma backed the claim of Magnus of Norway.

On Easter Sunday, 1043, Edward was formally crowned. He lost no time repaying his mother for her hatred. The Anglo-Saxon Chronicle tells the story:

> Fourteen days before St. Andrew's Mass [November 16th] the king was advised to ride from Gloucester, and in his company the Earls Leofric, Godwin, and Siward with their followers, to Winchester, unawares upon the lady Emma. And they bereaved her of all the treasures that she possessed, which were incalculable, because before that she had been very hard with the king her son, insomuch that she had done less for him than he wished, both before he was king and also after.

Edward wore the crown, but Earl Godwin called the tune. "He had been to such an extent exalted," says the chronicle of Florence of Worcester, "as if he had ruled the King and all England."

Edward had no reason to love this powerful Earl of Wessex who had won such a position. Godwin, after all, had been involved in the treacherous blinding and slaying of Edward's brother, Alfred the Atheling. Even Harthacnut, who profited from Alfred's death, had accused Godwin of plotting the deed. (Godwin soothed Harthacnut by presenting him with a splendid warship armed with eighty fighting men, and swore a mighty oath that he had had no part in the blinding of the prince.) Yet Edward had no choice. Godwin was the most powerful man in the kingdom, including the king himself. Swallowing any anger he may have felt over the murder of his brother, Edward continued Godwin in power, except for their quarrel of 1051, when the Earl of Wessex was driven for a short while into exile.

The quarrel came about this way. A Norman count, Eustace of Boulogne, husband of Edward's sister, had come to England for a visit. While in the town of Dover, Eustace's knights had become embroiled in a drunken quarrel with the men of Dover. Twenty citizens died, and nineteen of Eustace's retinue.

Eustace was outraged, though it seems his men provoked the brawl. He protested to Edward, who reacted typically. Dover lay under the jurisdiction of Earl Godwin, and Edward ordered Godwin to punish Dover with fire and sword for daring to attack the Norman guests.

Godwin refused. He had been smoldering long enough over the influence of the Normans on Edward. Now he would not destroy English homes for the sake of an offended Norman count. Instead, he defied Edward and mustered his troops for battle against the king. Civil war threatened.

Powerful as he was, Godwin could not successfully defy the King of England. Edward called out every soldier in the kingdom against the rebellious earl, and Godwin was forced to flee into exile, along with his sons. But in less than a year Godwin was back in England. The breach between him and Edward was healed, and Godwin was as powerful as ever.

After Godwin's death his son Harold, Earl of Wessex, played the same role in the kingdom. Edward had married Harold's sister, and openly recognized Harold as the most important earl in England. As Edward's life waned, Harold's strength grew—so that, as we have already seen, Harold Godwinsson was able to make himself England's king within a day of Edward's death.

After Edward's passing, myths grew up about him. Monks wrote biographies telling of his piety and saintliness, and dubbed him Edward the Confessor. (They were using the old meaning of the word, equivalent to "saint.") Miracles supposedly took place at his tomb. In 1161 Edward was formally sainted. This weak-willed, pink-faced man—who plundered his own mother's treasures, confirmed in power the probable slayer of his own brother, and fell upon the beasts of the field with bloody vengeance—was no more of a saint than anyone else of his times. Yet he was venerated for centuries after his death. Why?

Because he was a symbol. He was the last Old-English king to hold his throne without dispute, the last of the royal line of Cerdic and Alfred to be king. After him, for nine months, ruled a man not of royal blood, and then dark-haired strangers came to reign over England forever.

So Edward was revered not for what he had been, but for what he symbolized. The common people of England —the peasants and small knights, the Anglo-Saxons groaning under the heel of their Norman conquerors—made a saint out of Edward so that they might look back to a time when an Englishman ruled England. They had little else over which to rejoice. So thoroughly was the Old-English line of kings blotted out that when a new Edward came to the throne of England in 1272, he called himself not Edward IV (though he ruled after Edward the Elder, Edward the Martyr, and Edward the Confessor) but Edward I. The slate had been wiped clean.

It is a tangled tale of betrayals and bloodshed, of flashing swords and flying lances, of Harolds and Sweyns and Edwards, that we have here. Bold men stood face to face, fighting like demons for the right to rule. Harsh times, harsh men, and not a pretty story—but out of the crucible of 1066 came a new nation, a new breed of men, a new kingdom that would tower high as the clouds in Europe's destinies.

III

TWO HAROLDS AND WILLIAM

THREE MEN, ABOVE ALL OTHERS, SHAPED the events of that dark year of 1066. An Englishman, a Norman, and a Norwegian they were, and, strangely, in the veins of all three pulsed the blood of the Vikings. One—Harold Hardrada of Norway—was Viking pure. One—William of Normandy—was Viking turned Frenchman. One—Harold of England—was Viking mixed with Saxon. There was the chill of the north about all three.

Harold of England, the Earl of Wessex, was a tall man but slender, with the fair golden hair and blue eyes of his people. He looked younger than his years, men said. Born while Cnut was King of England, Harold was about forty when he ascended that throne himself.

He was the second of the many sons of Godwin of Wessex, that violent, power-hungry man. Of Godwin himself we know little, and of Godwin's father Wulfnoth even less —except that Wulfnoth, in 1009, while commanding part of England's royal fleet against the Danes, turned pirate and plundered like a Viking. The only word we have of Godwin's rise to power comes from an ancient Norse poem, the *Knytlinga Saga*, which deals with the deeds of Cnut.

The saga tells us that Earl Ulf, Cnut's brother-in-law, was leading a party of Danes against the English troops of Edmund Ironside. Pursuing some fugitives hotly into a thick wood, Ulf was separated from his men, and as night fell he realized he was lost. He wandered until morning. The breaking of dawn found him in a field, where a tall boy was driving sheep. Ulf went to the boy, and asked him his name.

"I am called Godwin," the boy replied. "But art thou one of Cnut's men?"

"I am certainly one of his warriors," answered Ulf. "But how far is it hence to our ships?"

"I do not know," said young Godwin, "how you Danes can expect help from us. You have not deserved it."

Ulf nevertheless said, "I will however ask of thee to help me find our ships."

Answered the boy: "Thou hast gone straight away from them, and far inland across wild forests. The men of Cnut are not very much liked by the people here, and for good reason, for the slaughter yesterday is known in the neighborhood. Neither thou nor any other of his men will be spared if captured; and if anyone help you the same fate awaits him. But I think thou art a good man."

Earl Ulf took a gold ring from his hand and said, "I will give thee this ring if thou wilt guide me to our men."

Godwin looked at him a while and said slowly, "I will not take the ring, but I will try to guide thee to thy men, and will rather have the reward thou thinkest right if I can give thee some help. But if I cannot help thee I deserve no reward."

Godwin took the Danish earl to his father's farm and gave him food and drink. That night Godwin and Ulf rode toward the ships, and the boy led Ulf safely back to his men. Then, says the saga, "The earl seated Godwin in the high-seat at his side, and treated him in everything like himself or his son, and shortly gave him in marriage his sister Gytha; and with the aid and advice of Ulf, King Cnut gave Godwin an earldom for the sake of Earl Ulf, his brother-in-law."

It is a fine story, and, like many of the stories in these old Norse sagas, it is probably more colorful than true. In one way or another, though, young Godwin did come to Earl Ulf's attention, and through Ulf became a favorite of Cnut's, and an earl of England.

Godwin had five sons and a daughter. The daughter, Edith, married King Edward and lived on into old age as the respected widow of the Confessor. The five sons, though, all died young, and died by violence.

Eldest of the five was Sweyn, who would in the normal course of events have succeeded Godwin as Earl of Wessex, and who might very well have become King of England. But Sweyn was a tempestuous, pleasure-loving man who committed outrage after outrage, until finally in 1048 he was banished from England. He came back a year later with a fleet, accompanied by two of his cousins, Sweyn and Boern Estrithson, nephews of Godwin's wife. They descended on England as pirates, but Beorn was killed, Sweyn Estrithson escaped in defeat, and Sweyn Godwinsson was banished again. The twelfth-century chronicle of William of Malmesbury notes:

Sweyn being of a perverse disposition, and faithless to the king, oftentimes disagreed with his father and his brother Harold: and afterwards proving a pirate, he stained the virtues of his ancestors with his robberies upon the seas. Last of all, being guilty unto himself of the murder of his kinsman Bruno . . . he traveled unto Jerusalem as a pilgrim: and in his return home, being taken by the Saracens, was beaten, and wounded unto death.

With the disgrace and early death of Sweyn, Harold came into prominence as Godwin's heir. He weathered the crisis of 1051–52, when he and Godwin were banished, and when he returned he became more powerful than ever. Succeeding his father as unofficial "under-king" to Edward, Harold gained experience in the arts of government and those of warfare.

For thirteen years Harold ruled in all but title, and ruled wisely with justice, so say the chronicles. During those years England was greatly troubled with warfare to the west in Wales, where unruly descendants of the Britons had long maintained their independence. Gruffyd ap Llewellyn, King of North Wales, was the chief troublemaker, aided and abetted by Alfgar, a young English nobleman whom Harold had made Earl of East Anglia. Alfgar and Gruffyd sacked Herefordshire in western England in 1055. Harold led an army against them, defeated Gruffyd, and captured Alfgar. Typical of Harold's generosity, he offered the rebellious Alfgar a pardon and restored him to his rank.

Gruffyd remained troublesome. He continued to harry western England. And in 1058 Alfgar—now Earl of Mercia—joined the Welshman again. It looked as though Alfgar might make war against Harold and King Edward, but again Harold's wisdom prevailed. Alfgar was pacified and made no further trouble before his death in 1062.

There was still Gruffyd to deal with. Harold carried the war into Wales now. Instead of using heavily armed mounted troops against the Welsh guerrilla fighters, Harold now adopted their own tactics. He sent fast-moving archers and swordsmen into Wales, and drove the Welshmen back into their mountain fastnesses. In a dramatic mid-winter raid, Earl Harold plunged deep into Wales, to Gruffyd's own seat at Rhuddlan, and captured the town, the king's treasures, his ships, and very nearly Gruffyd himself. The following spring—it was 1064—Harold raided Wales from the sea while his brother Tostig marched inland from the English border. Gruffyd was defeated in battle after battle, chased from town to town, until his own people turned on him and killed him. Harold sent Gruffyd's head and the gilded beaked figurehead of his ship to King Edward in token of the victory. Wales was subdued, and Harold was triumphant. He had learned much of warfare during his campaigns against Gruffyd, and had proved his bravery as well as his strategic skill on the battlefield.

At this, the time of Harold's greatest success, Edward the Confessor had less than two years to live. The old king had grown too feeble and ill to hunt, and had withdrawn almost completely from the outer world. He spent his days at prayer, used what little energy he had to supervise the building of his abbey at Westminster, and was quite content to let Earl Harold run the kingdom.

To all in England it seemed a foregone conclusion that Harold would one day, very soon, be king. True, Harold Hardrada, the King of Norway, thought he had a claim on the throne. So did Sweyn Estrithson, the nephew of Cnut, who had once gone raiding with his cousin Sweyn Godwinsson and who now was King of Denmark. But no one took the claims of those two very seriously except themselves. And, of course, there was Edgar the Atheling, young grandson of Edmund Ironside, but few were willing to back his claim either.

In the duchy of Normandy, just southward from England across the narrow Channel, Duke William, too, thought he had a claim to the English throne. Until 1064 it was a very shaky claim indeed. But in that year, as we will shortly see, a strange event took place that sent William's stock shooting high, and brought that of Harold of Wessex low.

THE NORMANS, though they spoke the French language and lived in what is now France, were not of French blood. They were Vikings out of Norway, sea raiders who had settled down.

In the year 911 a Viking named Rolf (or Rollo) raided his own country of Norway. A Norse saga tells us that Rolf was "a great Viking, and so large that no horse could carry him, so that he walked wherever he went, and for this reason he was called Rolf the Ganger (Rolf the Walker)." Harold Fairhair, King of Norway, outraged at Rolf the Ganger's piratical ways, banished him from his kingdom.

Rolf and his companions set out in their *drakkars*, or dragon ships, on a campaign of plunder on the seas. They headed around the north coast of Scotland in their red and black ships with high bows and sterns, and, looting as they went, sailed southward toward what is now France.

These men of the cold north found themselves coasting

along a green and fertile land. They sailed up the Seine to Jumièges, burning and robbing each town along the way, until they reached the rich, important cathedral city of Rouen. As they clustered outside the walls, ready to attack and destroy, the Archbishop of Rouen came forth and offered to surrender the city. Peacefully, Rolf's Norsemen entered Rouen.

It became their capital, and they struck out at the surrounding territory in raid after raid. They besieged Paris and Chartres, destroyed many towns, laid waste the farmland. The French people cried out for mercy. The King of France, Charles the Simple, agreed to negotiate with Rolf and his men.

Charles offered to give Rolf the title of count, and to grant him all the land he had already seized. In return Rolf was to acknowledge the King of France as his lord and master, was to become a Christian, and was to cease his attacks on other parts of France. To seal the agreement Rolf would take as his wife Gisele, the king's daughter.

The Viking agreed to all but one point. It was customary for a vassal, when acknowledging the gift of lands, to kneel before the king and kiss his foot. This Rolf refused to do. "Never will I bend the knee before any man, or kiss the foot of any man!" the giant Viking boomed.

The French insisted on the ritual. Rolf signaled to one of his men to pay the homage in his place. Without bending his knee, the warrior seized the king's foot and lifted it so high that Charles tumbled on to his back! The foot was duly kissed; Charles decided not to show anger; and the Norsemen were formally installed as vassals of the King of France.

The decades passed. Rolf, now a Christian and wearing the Christian name of Robert, put off his piratical ways.

The Norsemen gradually came to call themselves Normans and their district Normandy. They forswore paganism, became devout Christians, and built new churches and abbeys to replace those they had sacked. They gradually abandoned their harsh Norse language and spoke French instead, though with a rough Viking accent. After Rolf, ruled his son, William Longsword, and then William's son, Richard I, called the Fearless. Richard had many children, including Emma, who wed first King Ethelred and then King Cnut, and Richard, surnamed the Good, who became Duke Richard II of Normandy.

The chronicler William of Malmesbury tells us what sort of men these Normans were:

> They live in large castles; envy their equals; wish to excel their superiors; and plunder their subjects though they defend them from others. They are faithful to their lords though a slight offense renders them perfidious. They weigh treachery by its chance of success, and change their sentiments with money. They are, however, the kindest of nations, and they esteem strangers of equal honor with themselves.

Duke Richard II had three sons and three daughters. The sons quarreled among themselves. The eldest, who became Duke Richard III, ruled only a short while and then died of poisoning. There were those who said his brother Robert had had a hand in the crime, but Robert became duke none the less. Men called him Robert the Magnificent. He was a hearty, flamboyant man of huge appetites and gusty ways. Bold in battle, he went to war to aid Henry, King of France, who was in danger of losing his throne; he went to war on a similar errand for Baldwin,

Count of Flanders; and he mounted an unsuccessful invasion on behalf of his cousin Alfred, Emma's son, who claimed the throne of England then held by Cnut.

Robert was only seventeen, and not yet duke, when in 1027 he fell in love with Arlette of Falaise, a tanner's daughter. The story goes that Arlette was washing linens in a little stream that goes by the foot of Falaise Castle when Count Robert rode by and spied her. She became the mistress of the young nobleman, though never his wife.

In 1028 a son was born to them and named William. Across in England, Earl Godwin's wife Gytha was nursing a child of her own that year, called Harold.

Duke Richard III died, and Count Robert became Duke Robert the Magnificent. He took a wife—Estrith, sister of King Cnut of England—but no children were born to them, and Robert sent her away. His only child was William, the son of the tanner's daughter. Though he had been born out of wedlock, William was considered to be the heir to the dukedom of Normandy. An illegitimate duke was nothing new to the Normans. William Longsword, Richard the Fearless, and Richard the Good had all been born of unblessed unions.

When William was only about seven, Robert the Magnificent set out on his greatest adventure. Taking with him a handful of knights, he journeyed across Europe on a pilgrimage to Jerusalem. The contradictions in Duke Robert are shown by the way he traveled: barefoot, as befit a humble pilgrim, but riding a mule shod with solid gold.

The Holy Land's heat and its strange diseases laid Duke Robert low. A fever took him in Jerusalem, and he sent word back to Normandy of his illness, not without a flair of his old vigor: "Tell them at home that I am being carried off to Paradise by four black fiends."

The duke died in Asia Minor in 1035 at the age of twenty-five, and his title descended to the boy William. Even in childhood William had shown signs of his future greatness. A story said that soon after his birth he was set down to rest on a heap of white straw and began to clutch and pull at the straw until his pudgy hands were full. His nurses pointed to this as a token that he was destined "to amass and to acquire."

First, though, he had to make his dukedom his own. Christians the Normans may have been, but they had never forgotten their turbulent Viking ancestry. Rolf was not the only Norman who disliked bending the knee. Duke Robert, and the five Norman dukes before him, had held sway by the sheer force of their personalities and the strength of their swords. With Robert's death, though, the Norman barons' oaths of allegiance to Duke Robert were dissolved, and each man returned to his castle to work feverishly on his own behalf. Murder and revolt swept Normandy. Baron struck down baron. Robert had left his young son in the hands of loyal protectors, all of whom perished violently. Gilbert of Brionne, the boy's guardian, was murdered in view of witnesses by Robert of Giroye, a vengeful baron. Thurold, William's tutor, was killed soon after. Osbern, another guardian of the young duke, was stabbed to death while he shared his bed with William, and the boy woke up covered with the faithful Osbern's blood. William's uncle, Count Alain of Brittany, was poisoned in 1040.

Somehow William himself survived. The boy eluded assassins, chose loyal counselors, and grew toward manhood. He stored up for future settlement the wrongs committed against him and against his guardians. In bloody times Normandy was the bloodiest of lands, lacking as it did a single strong leader to keep feuding barons from one another's throats. William's enemies one by one eliminated each other in brutal, bitter warfare of Norman against Norman. Several plots against William's life miscarried only at the last moment. Then William turned to Henry, King of France, whom his father Duke Robert had helped to keep his throne. At William's pleading, Henry returned the favor; French soldiers came to William's aid. In 1047, when he was nineteen or twenty, William led troops into battle for the first time.

He subdued the rebellious Norman barons, distinguishing his name in battle. A thousand knights met at Val-es-Dunes, and the hills rang that day with the sound of sword smiting shield, of lance clanging against armor, of the Norman battlecry of *"Diex aie"* (God helps), the French roar, "Montjoye and Saint Denis," even a few Viking shouts to Thor and Odin.

The most important rebel leader was Ralph of Bayeux. Astride a great horse, William hacked his way through rebel knights toward Ralph to do single combat. At last one warrior alone guarded Ralph: a stalwart swordsman named Hardrez. The young duke faced the doughty Hardrez and struck a fierce blow of his sword that slashed through the rebel's coat of mail and left him dead on the spot. Ralph of Bayeux, seeing this, turned and fled from the field. William carried the day.

It was the turning point of his career. From then on the Normans bowed the knee to Duke William. He did not spend his days in peace, though, for other enemies remained. William became involved in prolonged campaigns against his neighbor, Geoffrey, Count of Anjou, called Geoffrey the Hammer. Duke William carried the war into Geoffrey's lands, reconquering territory that had once been Norman but had slipped into the possession of the counts of Anjou.

During these campaigns William committed a dark act that was not in keeping with his character. Although on the battlefield he dealt death lightheartedly, he disliked killing in cold blood—so much so that it pained him to put a criminal to death. Yet in this one case he showed himself capable of great cruelty.

It was at the siege of Alençon, a town on Norman soil that had given itself over to Anjou. William was hated there, and the rebellion against him in earlier years had been led by men of Alençon. When he came to liberate Alençon, William found a rude welcome. The men of the city had spread the skins of newly killed oxen on the walls of a guardhouse overlooking a bridge into the town. Beating on the hides with sticks, they cried, "Hides! Hides! Hides for the Tanner!"

It was a jeering, mocking reference to William's illegitimate birth and to his mother's father, the humble tanner of Falaise. William was infuriated. He swore to take vengeance on the mockers. His soldiers built a pyre of logs in front of the guardhouse and set fire to it; the guardhouse collapsed in flames and its defenders surrendered. At William's orders the hands and feet of the thirty-two defenders were lopped off and flung over the walls of the castle of Alençon—with the warning that the rest of the town faced the same fate.

Horrified, Alençon surrendered without resistance, and William repossessed it. But the callousness with which he treated the mocking men of the guardhouse haunted his name long afterward.

After Geoffrey of Anjou had been defeated, William faced a new enemy: Henry, King of France. Although he bore a resounding title, King Henry actually ruled only a small part of what is now France. Most of the country was in the hands of powerful nobles, such as the Duke of Normandy, the Count of Anjou, and the Duke of Burgundy. In theory, these men were vassals of the King of France. In actuality, they were vassals in name only, and went their own way with little heed for King Henry.

Henry had survived by playing one duke off against another. When Geoffrey of Anjou had grown too powerful, Henry had backed William of Normandy. But now William himself emerged as a strong leader, a threat to the king. In 1054 King Henry allied himself with Geoffrey of Anjou against Duke William. He declared that the original grant of Normandy to Rolf the Ganger by Charles the Simple was null and void, and he announced that he would march into Normandy to reclaim it as a direct possession of the French crown.

It was a grave test for Duke William. Henry formed an army made up of men from many provinces of France who had reason to dislike the Normans, men from Anjou and Maine, from Burgandy and Aquitaine. He divided the army into two forces, one on the left bank of the Seine, the other on the right, planning a pincer movement that would crush Normandy and the Norman capital of Rouen.

The French met with early success. They marched deep into Normandy, burning and plundering the villages in their path. The army on the right bank rested one night at the town of Mortemer, and there feasted and drank heavily to celebrate their victories. While the French slept soundly after their revelry, a Norman army under William's half-brother, Robert of Mortain, stole upon them, encircled the town, and set it afire. The surprised French were slaughtered almost to the last man.

King Henry, meanwhile, was encamped on the left bank, and William's army was not far away. During the night news came to William of the victory of his other force at Mortemer. Instead of doing battle with King Henry, William chose a different strategy. He sent Ralph of Tosny, a knight with the voice of a trumpet, to steal toward the sleeping French camp.

Ralph took a position on a cliff overlooking the French. Then his voice boomed out in the quiet of the night: "I am Ralph of Tosny," he cried, "and I bring you direful news. Wake up, you have slept too long. Go and bury your friends. They all lie dead at Mortemer!"

The French awoke and milled about in confusion. Soon after came messengers from the other army, confirming the news of the ghostly voice. Hastily King Henry called his men together. They broke camp in the darkness and fled back toward Henry's kingdom. By morning there were no French soldiers in Normandy but prisoners and corpses.

Shaken, the French king made peace with his mighty vassal, but three years later Henry of France and Geoffrey of Anjou were again in league against William. A second time they invaded; a second time William allowed enemy soldiers to enter Normandy; a second time he cut them to pieces. In the climactic battle William unveiled a secret weapon: the archers of Normandy, men whose twanging bows could strike men dead from afar. At a time when men fought with sword, spear, or battle-ax, the Norman archers were deadly beyond compare. Henry and Geoffrey never again invaded Normandy. They both died in 1060, and from that year onward William had no fear of losing Normandy. Little more than thirty years old, he had been duke for a quarter of a century. He had prevailed over enemies within and without Normandy. For the first time, now, his dukedom was at peace.

The restless William was now free to turn toward an old ambition of his. He could at last attempt to fulfil his dream of becoming King of England.

In William's boyhood two English princes, his cousins Alfred and Edward, dwelled at the Norman court at Rouen. We have already seen how Alfred met a violent fate and how Edward became England's monarch. And we have seen the visit of 1051 of Duke William to King Edward.

Godwin and Harold of Wessex were then in exile, and no one could foresee that they would return triumphantly soon afterward. William met with Edward, and one of the subjects they discussed must certainly have been the succession to the English throne. William always maintained that at their meeting of 1051 Edward had promised him, "You shall have the crown after me."

Be that as it may, Harold returned to England and made himself as powerful in that land as his father Godwin had been. And William, bedeviled by enemies at home, was in no position to think much about a foreign throne.

By 1060, though, William's enemies were dead or defeated. And Edward the Confessor was aging rapidly, so that soon England would need a new king. William, mindful of Edward's nine-year-old promise, hoped to fill the vacancy himself.

At thirty-two, William was a majestic, kingly figure. Tall

and broad-shouldered, muscular of arm and thigh, William's hair was jet-black, and he wore no beard, shaving not only his face but the back of his head, after the Norman fashion. A massive, craglike man whose deep, hoarse voice could be heard above the wildest din of battle, William wielded a bow that no other man was strong enough to bend. "No knight under heaven," his enemies admitted, "is William's peer." Half pirate, half statesman, William was crude and rough, yet deeply religious, a builder of abbeys as well as of castles. A concern for law and order and justice occupied him, yet at the same time, a chronicler writes, "So also was he a very stern and a wrathful man, so that none durst do anything against his pleasure." He brought order to Normandy for the first time in thirty years, establishing a code of harsh but just laws, putting an end to the strife of baron against baron, and, except for his moment of rage at Alençon, conducting himself always with a moderation that set him apart from most of the warriors of that fiery era.

He had taken a wife about 1052, Matilda, daughter of the Count of Flanders. Pope Leo IX had opposed the marriage for political reasons, but William, though a pious man, had defied the pope on this one matter and eventually was able to have his way. Matilda gave William the sons that any ruler needed: first Robert, later Duke of Normandy; then Richard, who died in youth from a hunting accident; William, called Rufus the Red, who became King William II of England; and Henry, who also held England's throne as Henry I.

Normandy was too small to hold a man like William. England beckoned. He knew, of course, that Harold of Wessex would attempt to seize the throne after Edward died. But William had little regard for Harold, or for anyone else who stood in his way. He believed beyond hesitation in his own military prowess.

With good reason. William of Normandy was a military genius, a general to rank with Alexander the Great and Julius Caesar and Hannibal. Like all great generals, he understood the importance of innovation in military tactics. The man who thought of something new—and made it work—had the advantage of surprise, the greatest weapon of all.

William revolutionized military tactics, adopting all the most efficient methods of his time and combining them to great advantage. In his day the English still fought on foot, hewing at each other with sword or battle-ax. The Normans fought on horseback, thrusting with lance against the milling enemies far below, scattering them before the plunging hoofs of their steeds. Backing up the Norman cavalry came the archers, whose swift shafts could terrorize an army in a matter of moments.

Against the Norman forces no enemy could stand—so William had learned in a lifetime of waging war. And so, William hoped, Harold would discover also, if it ever came to a passage of arms between William's men and Harold's.

BETWEEN 1060 AND 1064 William bided his time, occupying himself with mopping up the last resistance to his rule in Normandy and Maine, while Harold of Wessex campaigned in Wales and proved to be no mean general himself. In the summer of 1064, however, a strange and stunning thing happened. Harold, "under-king" of England and the man next in line for the English throne, fell a captive into Duke William's hands!

How it happened is shrouded in mystery. There are several versions of the story, handed down to us by different chroniclers, some Norman, some English. We cannot be sure which version is the correct one. At any rate, toward the end of the summer of 1064 Earl Harold set out from the harbor of Bosham in Sussex. Some say he was simply taking a pleasure cruise in the English Channel, others that he was on a diplomatic mission to Flanders or some other European capital, or even that Edward the Confessor had sent him to pay homage to Duke William.

Two, or perhaps three, ships set out. They were ships in the Viking style, long and brightly colored, with gay sails of rainbow hues. In the bow of one stood Harold himself, a tall, slim, fair-haired figure, his nearly invisible blond mustache glittering as he looked eastward into the rising sun. He carried a falcon on his wrist and a small dog under one arm as his little fleet moved out into the Channel.

The expedition begun in such gaiety ended in catastrophe. Harold was driven southward by a sudden storm; his ships were forced upon the French coast near Abbeville and wrecked. A fisherman who had once been to England recognized the earl as he stumbled ashore, and bore the news to Count Guy of Ponthieu, whose territory this was.

Count Guy, it appears, made a practice of imprisoning the victims of shipwrecks and holding them for ransom. He rode down to the shore and carried Harold off to his castle at Beaurain, informing Harold that he would be his "guest" until a proper ransom was paid. The English earl was cast into a dungeon.

But Guy had landed a big fish indeed, and word was swift in reaching Duke William of Count Guy's prize. Now, Guy of Ponthieu was one of the barons who had

Harold embarks for Normandy

fought against William in earlier years. He had been captured at the rout of Mortemer, and William had held him prisoner for two years, releasing him only upon a vow of loyalty. William proceeded to invoke that vow now. He sent messengers to Count Guy, ordering him to release Earl Harold into William's custody.

The count, expecting a handsome ransom, grumbled at this. But he feared William's wrath, and after some reluctance he had Harold's fetters removed. Harold was taken to the castle of Eu, near the border of Normandy and Ponthieu, where William met him.

They rode together to William's capital of Rouen. Despite the unusual circumstances under which Harold had arrived in Normandy, William chose, outwardly at least, to regard Harold's presence as a state visit and Harold as his invited guest. He showered hospitality on the shipwrecked

Englishman, wining and dining him in great state. The two men seem to have gotten along well—the fair, youthful-looking Englishman and the dark, massive Norman. They were both men of regal bearing, both had won distinction in battle, both enjoyed the pleasures of the tournament and the chase. William took Harold from town to town in his domain, to Caen and Bayeux, to Fecamp and Lillebonne. He proudly displayed his fine Arab steeds; he caused knightly contests to be staged for Harold's amusement; he gave banquet after banquet.

Harold was perhaps eager to return to England. But he could not seem to spurn William's hospitality. Weeks dragged on into months, and still Harold remained at the Norman duke's court. William appeared determined to make a fast friend of Harold, to rivet a firm comradeship.

William also chose to display the strength of his army—perhaps by way of warning Harold of the dangers of warring with Normandy. He invited Harold to join him on a military expedition to nearby Brittany, where Count Conan was harrying the Norman borders.

The English earl rode out with the Norman duke and his troops. The company of knights came to the River Couësnon, marking the boundary between Normandy and Brittany, and as they forded the river several Norman horsemen became mired in quicksand. Without hesitating, Harold dismounted. Stretching a long Norman shield over the sands, the Englishman ventured onto it, extended a hand to the nearest Norman, and by sheer physical force hauled him free of the mire. One by one Harold dragged all the entrapped Normans clear—while William, standing by, watched with interest this display of Harold's bravery and strength.

The expedition continued onward, only to find that Count Conan had fled. William ventured deep into Brittany and besieged Conan finally at the town of Dinan. Here, after a brief siege, Conan surrendered and swore an oath of fealty to William. The campaign was over. To celebrate the victory, William proposed to knight Harold on the battlefield.

England did not have such a custom, but among the Normans it was a serious matter indeed. By "giving arms" to Harold, William was—in his own eyes—establishing himself as Harold's overlord, and Harold was vowing an oath of loyalty to William. Harold knelt before William in the formal ceremony and was knighted. The friendship between the two was at its closest.

When they returned to Normandy, William at last spoke what had been on his mind since Harold's unexpected arrival. In all cordiality Duke William said, "When King Edward and I once lived like brothers under the same roof, he promised that if ever he became King of England, he would make me heir to his throne. Harold, I wish that thou wouldst assist me to realize this promise."

The chronicler who set this story down was a Norman, and he tells us that Harold immediately agreed to help William obtain the English throne after Edward's death. This seems a little hard to believe, since Harold had royal ambitions of his own.

But Harold was far from home and at William's mercy in Normandy. Quite likely the Englishman realized that the safest and wisest thing to do was to show a friendly face to William. Later, once back in England, he could always reconsider his promise.

So it may have happened that Harold did actually prom-

William knights Harold

ise to aid William. They also seemed to have discussed an arrangement by which one of Harold's sisters would marry a Norman baron, and Harold himself would marry William's daughter Adelisa. This, too, appeared agreeable to Harold.

William had one more card to play, and he played it craftily. At Duke William's castle at Bayeux there convened the grand council of barons and bishops of Normandy, and here William maneuvered Harold into repeating his pledges in public.

Seated on his throne, wearing a golden circlet as his crown, carrying in his hand the great sword of state, William bade Harold step before him. Between the Norman and the Englishman there rested a chest covered with cloth of gold, and atop the chest there lay a Bible.

Taken off guard, Harold could only gape dumfounded as William said, "Earl Harold, I require thee, before this noble assembly, to confirm by oath the promises which thou hast made me, to assist me in obtaining the crown of England after King Edward's death, to marry my daughter Adelisa, and to send me thy sister, that I may give her in marriage to one of my barons."

Harold was trapped. He could not renounce in public the promises he had privately made to William. He had no choice but to swear. He laid his hand on the Bible, and, the old Norman chronicler says, "when Harold placed his hand on it, the hand trembled, and the flesh quivered."

Harold swore upon his oath that he would take Adelisa to wife, would deliver up England to William, and would do all in his power to assist William thereafter, so help him God.

"God grant it!" the Norman barons cried.

Harold swears upon his oath

Harold rose from his knees and stepped back. William had a jolting surprise in store for the English earl. He caused the cloth of gold to be lifted, and beneath it lay a chest, and within the chest were the bones and relics of the Norman saints. William had had Normandy scoured for sacred relics, and Harold had unknowingly sworn his oath on them.

To us it seems like pure decoration. A man's word is his word, whether it is given in a simple declaration or sworn over a chest of old bones. In the eleventh century, though, an oath taken over the relics of saints was deemed irrevocable. To break it would be blasphemy.

How Harold felt about his oath, his later actions well show. He had been tricked by William, and, bones or no bones, he felt that the oath was not binding on him. Not only had it been obtained through deceit, but it had been imposed virtually by force, since Harold was really William's prisoner. Such an oath is no oath at all, Harold must have felt.

William, though, had what he wanted. He had compelled Harold to swear, before the Norman barons, to hand over England to him after Edward's death. The oath-taking ceremony served as the basis of William's claim to England. And, as we will see, William made good use of that oath when the time came to assemble his army of invasion.

Soon after the ceremony Harold was permitted to depart. He returned to England safely and told the tale of his long sojourn in Normandy to King Edward. The old king listened gravely to the story of the oath and the promise. But we do not know how he counseled Harold. All we know is that upon the king's death, a year and a half later, Harold chose to ignore his oath and to place himself on England's throne in defiance of Duke William's wrath.

THE THIRD WHO YEARNED TO RULE over England was Harold of Norway, Harold Hardrada. This is what a Norse saga of the twelfth century tells us about him:

> It was said by all that Harold Hardrada surpassed other men in wisdom and sagacity, whether a thing was to be done quick or in a long time, for himself or others. He was more weapon-bold than any man, as has been told. He was a handsome and majestic-looking man with auburn hair, an auburn beard and long mustaches; one eyebrow a little higher up than the other; large arms and legs and well shaped. His measure in height was three ells. [Six feet nine inches.] He was cruel towards his foes, and punished all offenses severely. He was very eager for rule, and all prosperous things. He gave his friends great gifts when he liked them well.

This giant Viking had had a glittering career of war, and he had seen more of the world than most men of his day. While his brother Olaf ruled in Norway, Harold Hardrada roved far to the east, to Byzantium, where he commanded the Varangian Guards at Constantinople. He fought in Sicily and in Africa, Greece and Italy, Bulgaria and the Holy Land. He saw action at Novgorod in distant Russia. He loved a Byzantine empress and put out the eyes of a Byzantine emperor. Wherever there was danger in the world, there could be found Harold Hardrada, towering a head taller than any man about him, hewing a bloody path with his enormous sword and his mighty battle-ax. He was the last of the great Norse heroes and one of the greatest of them all.

Harold Hardrada's brother Olaf had been thrust from the throne of Norway by that other doughty Viking, Cnut. Cnut had made his son Sweyn King of Norway after him, but Sweyn was disliked by the people, who rose up against him. Sweyn was driven out and Magnus, son of Olaf and nephew of Harold Hardrada, came to the throne.

It was King Magnus who had made the famous treaty with Harthacnut of England and Denmark by which if either king died without an heir, his kingdom should go to the other. When Harthacnut died soon after, however, Magnus was unable to claim his legacy. The throne of England went to Edward, son of King Ethelred and half-brother of Harthacnut. The throne of Denmark was seized by Sweyn Estrithson, son of Earl Ulf and Estrith, sister of Cnut. Magnus made a token claim of England's crown, but for the next five years devoted all his energy to an unsuccessful attempt to drive Sweyn Estrithson out of Denmark.

Magnus died in 1047. To the Norwegian throne came

his uncle, hard-bitten Harold Hardrada. He insisted that he had inherited Magnus's claim to the English crown by virtue of Magnus's treaty with Harthacnut.

For nearly twenty years Harold Hardrada asserted that claim without making any attempt to put it into force. The lofty Norseman was too busy making war on Denmark to be able to take on the much bigger task of attacking England. Viking strength was tempered in Harold Hardrada by unusual cunning. As an old saga relates, "He never fled from a battle, but often he took precautions when he had to do with an overwhelming force. All men who followed him in battle and warfare said that when he was in a great danger which came quickly upon him he would take the action which afterwards was seen by all to be the best."

In this case Harold Hardrada felt that his best path was to wait. He was in the prime of life and strong. King Edward of England was old and weak. And King Edward was well liked by his people. Any attempt to remove him from power would arouse the anger of the English. It would mean bloody war and the waste of Norwegian lives.

Far better to wait, Harold Hardrada thought. King Edward would not live forever. When he died, there would be no real heir to the English throne, and the Norwegians could make their move. A sudden invasion, a lightning swoop, and a Norse giant would be king in England. Harold Hardrada knew, of course, that Harold son of Godwin would stand in his way. But a man who had slain foes on all three continents of the known world had no fear of a slender English earl. Nor did dark Duke William of Normandy frighten the Viking. When the time came, Harold Hardrada believed, enemies would fall headlong as they had always fallen before him. England would be his.

Harold Hardrada waited. The years lengthened. King

Edward weakened but would not die. Harold Hardrada himself grew old. He was nearly fifty, though his strength was undiminished. And at last came the word for which he had been waiting. Old Edward was dead.

Onward to England!

IV

THE GATHERING CLOUDS

Harold of Wessex was still new to England's throne when a strange omen brightened the winter sky and struck fear into the hearts of his subjects. What the people thought was "a new star" gleamed briefly in the heavens, flashed through the night, and was gone.

They said it presaged disaster. We know today that it was simply Halley's comet, which is visible from earth about once every seventy-five years, but the English chose to interpret it as a sign of ill omen. Men watching in the fields looked up and pointed, marveling at the "star," and ran to bring the word to King Harold.

King Harold had more to perturb him than omens in the sky. Having at last gained the title that had been his in all but name for thirteen years, he had work aplenty to do. King Edward had shrugged off the responsibility of a ruler. He had made no laws, had avoided every decision. Harold,

Harold learns of the ominous "new star"

as "under-king" in Edward's reign, had lacked full authority to govern the land. Harold now had to undo the chaos wrought by a quarter of a century of Edward the Confessor's kindly but ineffectual rule.

Since he had taken the throne in January, King Harold knew that he had some months yet before he need fear a foreign invasion. Men did not make war in wintertime. Harold Hardrada of Norway, whose invasion of England had been dreaded for two decades, was now more of a threat than ever, but ice in the northern seas would hold him back till spring. William of Normandy also was reported to be planning an attack, but he, too, would wait for fairer weather.

"Little quiet did he enjoy the while that he wielded the kingdom," the Anglo-Saxon Chronicle says of Harold. He was in no enviable position, menaced as he was from two sides at once. But he lost little time in lamenting his danger. He had known the risks when he first mounted the throne. His task was to strengthen England, win the support of the nobles and the people, and ready his country for the onslaughts it faced.

He was busy, those months of January and February and March, 1066. Says the chronicler Florence of Worcester:

> He set to work to remove unjust laws, and to devise good ones, to make himself the patron of churches and monasteries. He was attentive and respectful to all ecclesiastical persons. He showed himself dutiful, courteous and kindly to all good men, but a terror to ill-doers. He bade his earls, governors and sheriffs arrest all who troubled the kingdom, and set himself energetically to provide for the defense of the country by land and by sea.

Although historians have little information about Harold's actual measures as king, the soundness of the English currency in 1066 indicates that the administrative machinery was well under Harold's control. In 1066 English coins were struck at forty-four different places in every part of England. All the coins had the same design, showing that they were struck by order of the central government at London. In less efficiently governed realms, local princelings often issued their own coinage. The coins of Harold showed the king, bearded and handsome, facing to the left and wearing his crown. The inscription was HAROLD REX ANGLORUM—"Harold, King of the Angles."

Although Harold seems to have been able to maintain order over most of England during his reign, he had some problems in the North. Northern England—Northumbria and Mercia—had never been altogether easy about the rule of the dynasty of Wessex. In those northern provinces there were still strong traditions of a time when local kings had ruled. Five hundred years before, the kings of Northumbria had been the most powerful in England, and three of them in succession, Edwin, Oswald, and Oswiu, had held the honorary title of *Bretwalda*, "ruler of all Britain." Mercia, too, had its great heroes, Ethelbald and Offa, whose long reigns stretched from 716 to 757 and from 757 to 796, respectively. In those days Wessex had been unimportant, a subject kingdom.

Those days were long gone. For more than two hundred years the descendants of Egbert of Wessex had ruled England, but for the interlude of Danish supremacy. Now Egbert's dynasty too was gone, but still a man from Wessex claimed to be king. The proud men of Northumbria and Mercia bitterly resented the dominance of the southerners.

In the early part of King Edward's reign, when Godwin was Earl of Wessex and told the king what to do, Leofric was Earl of Mercia and Siward was Earl of Northumbria. The families of both those men had suffered in the years that followed, and Godwin's family had risen at their expense.

Siward had died in 1055. His only son Waltheof was still a child, so the earldom passed to Godwin's family. The new Earl of Northumbria was Tostig, younger brother of Harold—a selfish, cruel man whom we will soon meet again.

Alfgar, the son of Earl Leofric of Mercia, objected to this change. As we have seen, Alfgar rebelled, joined forces with Gruffyd of Wales, and was eventually subdued by Harold. When Earl Leofric died, the great earldoms of England were realigned. Alfgar became Earl of Mercia, but much of his land was cut away and given to Gyrth, another of Godwin's sons. Thus by 1057 Godwin's family held every earldom in England except that of Mercia. After Alfgar's death in 1062, his son Edwin succeeded him as Earl of Mercia.

Tostig, Earl of Northumbria, was vastly unpopular among the people of the north, who had no love for the men of Wessex and preferred to be ruled by one of their own kind. In 1065 open rebellion broke out against Tostig. The rebels seized York, the most important town of Northumbria, and sacked Tostig's palace. With Harold's brother banished, the rebels held a solemn assembly and named a new earl themselves. They chose Morcar, the son of Alfgar and the brother of Earl Edwin of Mercia.

This was a bold defiance of King Edward and also of Harold, who was the real ruler. But, strangely, Harold did not go to his brother's defense. It was October, 1065, and Harold had recently returned from Normandy. Perhaps, with an eye toward the future, he did not want to go to war against Englishmen on behalf of a brother he knew to be wicked and arrogant. With the gesture of a true patriot Harold spared England from bloodshed. He agreed that Tostig would have to go.

It was decided that Morcar, whom the rebels had put in power, would remain Earl of Northumbria. Tostig would be banished. And there would be no reprisals against the rebels.

In this way Harold hoped to win the friendship of the people of northern England and of their leaders, the brothers Edwin and Morcar. But despite his willingness to sacrifice Tostig's ambitions, Harold gained little by his action. Edwin and Morcar, spurred on by their victory, became even more independent-minded than before, and in the final months of King Edward's rule the provinces of Mercia and Northumbria went their own way, little heeding the commands of the central government.

When Harold became king, he knew that he must certainly bring the two wealthy provinces back into harmony with the rest of England. So we see Harold, early in his reign, journeying to York to parley with Edwin and Morcar.

The two northern earls at first did not care to accept the brother of the hated Tostig as their king. They were jealous of all southerners, and especially jealous of the sons of Godwin. Although they did not themselves try to claim the English throne at any time Edwin and Morcar were unhappy about bowing to Harold Godwinsson.

Harold showed that he was a good diplomat. He brought with him to York the saintly, eloquent Bishop of Worcester, Wulfstan, who spoke to the earls. Wulfstan pointed out the dangers in which England stood. There in Normandy grumbled Duke William, plotting invasion. In Norway raged the titanic Harold Hardrada, dreaming of shedding English blood. Even Sweyn Estrithson, who had barely been able to hang onto his own crown in Denmark all these years, was talking about claiming the English throne! Was this a time for Englishman to quarrel with Englishman? Was this a time for disunity?

Wulfstan won the day. Edwin and Morcar grudgingly bowed the knee to King Harold. To seal the agreement Harold took as his wife Aldgyth, sister of Morcar and Edwin, and widow of Harold's old enemy, King Gruffyd of

Wales. Though Harold was now their brother-in-law, Edwin and Morcar still bore little love for him. That they would no longer oppose him did not mean they would actively support him.

It was in May, while Harold was still in York trying to win Edwin and Morcar's support, that the new king's troubles began in earnest. England was invaded.

It was the first of many invasions that the island kingdom would have to endure that year. The attacker, however, was not William of Normandy or Harold of Norway, nor was he Sweyn of Denmark.

He was Tostig, Harold's own brother.

TOSTIG IS THE DARKEST FIGURE of all the characters who played parts in the tragedy of 1066. The third of Godwin's sons, he was bold and self-confident, and his bravery was equaled only by his treachery. Unlike Harold, who was open and generous, Tostig was a schemer, a malcontent, who nurtured hatred in his bosom. Yet, strangely, old King Edward had loved Tostig dearly, and some said he favored him even above Harold himself.

The hot-headed Tostig was named by Edward to be Earl of Northumbria after Siward died, but the Northumbrians never loved him. They suspected him of having arranged the murder of Cospatric, a northerner who had a legitimate claim to the ancient earldom. For ten years Tostig ruled uneasily in Northumbria, but spent most of his time in the south, hunting at the side of King Edward.

Finally, in October, 1065, while Tostig was off on a hunting expedition again, his people rose against him, and, as we have seen, the rebellion ended in Tostig's banishment. At a meeting of the witan, Tostig rose and accused

Harold of having encouraged the rebellion in Northumbria himself in order to rid himself of a dangerous rival.

Harold denied this. The witan voted for Tostig's banishment. King Edward, Tostig's chief backer, was too weak to prevent it. Late in 1065, Tostig and his wife Judith, along with their children, left England to go into exile at the court of Judith's brother, Baldwin, Count of Flanders.

All during that bitter winter Tostig schemed against his brother. He remained in exile, though one Norse saga seems to say that he returned to England to see Harold crowned king. If he did so, it must have been a harsh sight for him.

Tostig brooded now on ways to bring his brother down. Such treachery was no hardship for Tostig, whose whole career had been marked by black deeds. A chronicler notes that in 1064, "in his own chamber in York, he slew by treachery Gamel, son of Orm, and Ulf, son of Dolfin, who had come to him under sworn safe-conduct."

He was too weak, though, to conquer Harold alone. He needed an ally—no great problem in that year when many men sought Harold's downfall.

Tostig went first to William of Normandy. The duke was smoldering with rage over Harold's accession to the kingship, and Tostig proposed a deal. William would provide him with a fleet and soldiers with which to invade England. If Tostig succeeded in overthrowing Harold, he would give the crown of England to William—but would keep the northern half of the island for himself, and the rank of Earl of Northumbria.

William does not seem to have taken kindly to Tostig's plot. Maybe the noble-minded William was disgusted with the traitorous Tostig, or perhaps the Norman duke simply did not feel like sharing England, which he claimed for his own, with anyone else. In any event, Tostig left Normandy dissappointed.

He turned next to Sweyn Estrithson of Denmark. Tostig and Sweyn were cousins, and many years before they had gone adventuring together. Tostig reminded Sweyn of those days. He stressed the fact that the Danish king's father, Earl Ulf, had been the brother of Tostig's mother, Gytha. And Ulf's wife, Estrith, had been the sister of King Cnut, ruler of England, Denmark, and Norway. On the one hand, Sweyn was related to Tostig; on the other, he had a distant claim to England's crown.

Tostig asked Sweyn for help in conquering England. Sweyn was not so minded. He suggested, instead, that Tostig settle in Denmark and take the title of earl.

Tostig answered, "I long to go back to England, to my homestead. I will give you all the help I can give in England if you will go there with the Danish host to win the land, as your uncle, Cnut the Great, did."

Sweyn was still unwilling. "I am much weaker than my kinsman Cnut," he replied. "I can scarcely defend Denmark against the Norwegians and Harold Hardrada. I had rather act moderately according to my strength than follow the deeds of my kinsman Cnut."

Tostig responded scornfully. "Maybe I shall search for friendship where it is far more undeserved," he declared. "I may find a chief who is less afraid to plan great things than thou, king."

Sweyn and Tostig parted, "and not on very friendly terms," the old saga relates. The rebellion-minded Englishman made yet another journey, this one to Norway and Harold Hardrada. Tostig told the Norwegian king of his travels, and of the rebuffs he had received from William and from Sweyn. He asked the Norseman to help him defeat Harold.

Crafty old Hardrada answered that his men were not thirsting to do battle under an English chief. "It is said that the English are not to be much trusted," the Viking boomed.

Tostig was bold enough to taunt the Norwegian king. Did he mean to slumber here in the north while Harold ruled England? England, Tostig insisted, would welcome Harold Hardrada joyfully. And he added with no show of modesty, "I lack nothing but the name of king to equal my brother Harold. All know that a greater warrior than thou has never been born in the northern lands, and it seems strange to me that thou didst fight fifteen years for Denmark and will not try for England, which is easy for thee to get."

Harold Hardrada pondered Tostig's words and finally offered the son of Godwin some encouragement. The record is unclear, but it seems that Tostig received money and perhaps some ships from Harold Hardrada—and possibly some backing from William of Normandy as well. In May of 1066 Tostig and his little armada gathered in a Norman port and set sail for England.

Their first stop was the Isle of Wight, just off England's southern coast. The islanders hailed Tostig as Godwin's son and King Harold's brother, without seeming to realize that he planned rebellion. They provided him with money and supplies. Tostig then sailed eastward along England's southern coast, plundering the towns of Kent.

When he reached the port of Sandwich, he was joined by Copsi, a suporter of his from Northumbria who had been exiled with Tostig in 1065. Copsi had come from the

Orkneys, islands belonging to Norway, with seventeen ships to add to Tostig's fleet.

King Harold had hurriedly returned from York when he heard of Tostig's invasion. He was in London when news came that Tostig had landed in Sandwich. Gathering a small force of picked soldiers, Harold hastened southward to deal with his unruly brother.

Tostig did not linger in Sandwich to do battle with Harold. He hired a number of sailors there and made off with some ships that had been in port. Now heading a fleet of sixty vessels, Tostig left port and sailed northward up England's east coast.

The invaders landed at the mouth of the Burnham River in Norfolk and burned several towns. Then they continued north to the mouth of the River Humber and landed on the southern bank. This was the province of Mercia, governed by Edwin, one of Tostig's bitterest foes. Tostig vented his rage on Edwin by sacking and looting town after town, slaying hundreds of innocent villagers, and doing great damage. Edwin, gathering an army, finally defeated Tostig and drove him out. He sailed northward again and tried to land in Morcar's earldom of Northumbria, but the Northumbrians thwarted him and forced him out to sea. At this point the men and ships Tostig had acquired in Sandwich deserted. Reduced to only a dozen small ships, Tostig took refuge with Malcolm, King of Scotland, a dedicated foe of England in general and of Earl Morcar of Northumbria in particular. Tostig stayed on as Malcolm's guest through the summer of 1066, licking his wounds. But before the leaves were falling from the trees, Tostig was in touch with Harold Hardrada again, plotting anew the downfall of King Harold of England.

So ended, ignominiously, the first invasion of England that year. King Harold had not needed to do battle himself. Edwin and Morcar had dealt with Tostig, not out of loyalty to Harold so much as to defend their own territories.

A far stronger enemy, meanwhile, was contemplating King Harold's doom.

DUKE WILLIAM OF NORMANDY had been in the ducal forest near Rouen, trying out a new bow, when a messenger ran to him with letters from England. Certain Normans living in London had sent word of Edward's death and Harold's seizure of the throne. The messenger had traveled fast. Only three days had elapsed since the coronation.

William's wrath was great. He canceled the hunt and stormed from the forest, returning in a towering rage to his palace. There he sat in the great hall, alone and silent, his head leaning against a pillar, his face black with anger. His barons, afraid to disturb him in his fury, held back, whispering tensely. Finally William Fitz-Osbern, one of the duke's closest friends, dared to approach. He advised William to shake off his fit of brooding, to arise and take action against the usurper Harold.

Duke William called his closest counselors together, and the most influential of all seems to have been Lanfranc, a wise and scholarly Italian priest who had come to hold great esteem in William's eyes. Lanfranc and William drafted a message to the new King Harold. In it Duke William bluntly reminded Harold of his oath of the year before, the oath which he had sworn "with his mouth, and his hand, upon good and holy relics."

The message to Harold went off swiftly, so that it reached Harold within ten days of King Edward's death.

William confers with his counselors

King Harold's reply was equally swift. Harold's words were bold and mocking.

"It is true," he told Duke William, "that I took an oath. But I took it under constraint. I promised what did not belong to me—what I could not in any way hold. My royalty is not my own. I could not lay it down against the will of the country, nor can I against the will of the country take a foreign wife. As for my sister, whom I promised to a Norman chief, she has died within the year. Does the Duke wish me to send her corpse?"

William sent a second message, a milder one. Instead of demanding that Harold resign the kingdom to him, the Norman simply asked that Harold publicly renew his pledge of loyalty to the Duke of Normandy. And to token the pledge, Harold must marry—as he had promised to do—Duke William's daughter. Otherwise, William threatened, he would raise an army and come against England with sword and lance.

Harold's reply made his stand bitingly clear. Not only would he defy William and keep his throne, but he would swear no loyalty. And as for the marriage to William's daughter—why, that was out of the question, for King Harold had just taken a wife, Aldgyth, sister of Edwin and Morcar!

William's pride was stung. War became inevitable.

It was winter, though, and no invasion would be possible for many months. And several steps remained before William could launch his attack. Powerful though he was, he could not act without the consent of his barons in so grave a matter.

The Norman duke's first step was to gain the support of the pope. As leader of Christendom, the pope had great political powers in that day, as well as his spiritual ones. At least in theory, every Christian owed allegiance to the pope as well as to his own ruler.

The powers of the pope, however, varied with the strength of the individual who held the Throne of St. Peter. When a weak pope ruled, hardly anyone beyond Rome itself paid much attention to him. A strong pope could enforce his will even over kings and dukes. England and Normandy, being geographically far removed from the pope's seat at Rome, often went their own way in defiance of the Holy Father. We have seen how Pope Leo IX had quarreled with Duke William over the duke's marriage, and finally had had to let William do as he pleased.

Leo IX was also pope when Godwin forced King Edward the Confessor to expel his Norman friends from power. Robert, the Archbishop of Canterbury and a Norman, was one of the victims of this purge. He was replaced by Stigand, a Saxon and a friend of Godwin's who, as we have noted, simultaneously held the post of Bishop of Winchester.

Pope Leo refused to approve such a shift. He was angered that Godwin should dare to expel an anointed archbishop of the church, and doubly angered that Stigand should try to hold two high church posts at once. So he summoned Stigand to Rome. Stigand wisely refused to go, and Pope Leo ordered him stripped of his churchly rank and excommunicated—that is, cut off from all the sacraments of the church.

Leo was in Rome, and Stigand in Canterbury. Protected by Godwin and later by Harold, Stigand went right on holding his rank, and there was nothing the pope could do about it. Leo IX died in 1054. Pope Victor II, who succeeded him, continued the excommunication of Stigand. And Stephen X, who became pope in 1057, did the same.

Stephen X died in 1058. At that time men contended for the papacy almost as violently as they did for worldly thrones. From April 1058 to January 1059 a usurper ruled Christianity, calling himself Pope Benedict X. Pope Benedict backed Stigand, and the English prelate hurried to Rome, where the new pope gave him the pallium, an archbishop's symbol of office.

Within a few months Benedict X was out of office. The new pope, Nicholas II, was of the old party. He promptly excommunicated Stigand once again, and his successor, Alexander II, maintained the same stand.

Alexander II was pope in 1066. William knew that he was angry with the English for permitting an excommunicated man to hold the highest church post in England, in defiance of Rome. William's messenger to Pope Alexander pointed out the following things:

That Harold supported Archbishop Stigand and had taken no steps to remove him from office. (Though Harold had taken care not to let Stigand perform the coronation ceremony!)

That Harold had profaned the relics of the holy saints by breaking his vow.

That Harold had usurped the throne of England in opposition to the wishes of God's anointed king, Edward, who had promised it to William.

That Harold had shared with his father Godwin guilt in two old crimes, the murder of Alfred the Atheling and the expulsion from England of the rightful Archbishop of Canterbury, Robert.

William's messenger also noted the devotion of the Norman duke to religion, citing the number of churches and abbeys William had built. Had Harold done the same? No. Harold showed little interest in affairs of religion.

Pope Alexander was extremely interested in William's arguments. He had reasons of his own for preferring William to Harold. He saw in it a way of bringing troublesome England more closely under papal control. The English priests were dreadfully independent of Rome in matters large and small, from the recognition of Stigand down to trifling elements of ritual. And in recent years they had been slow in sending to Rome the tribute known as Peter's Pence, which the pious King Cnut had first imposed on the English.

The pope and his cardinals held a formal hearing. Perhaps Harold was invited to attend, but certainly he did not care to come, since the outcome was inevitable. The pope gave William his full blessing to invade England. He declared Harold and all his followers excommunicated, and Harold stripped of the crown he had usurped. To William was given a diamond ring in which were set a hair and a tooth of St. Peter as a symbol of the support of God and the pope for his cause, and also a banner consecrated by the pope, which William was to unfurl on England's shores.

It was a shattering blow to Harold's hopes of maintaining his kingdom. His position in England was not seriously affected, since the men of that island had long been accustomed to defying the pope or any other foreign prince who tried to influence England's internal affairs. But now, in the eyes of all the Christians of Europe, Harold stood alone, and God was declared to be on William's side.

With the pope's blessing obtained, William now summoned the leaders of his realm. First came William's half-brothers, sons of his mother Arlette's second marriage: Robert of Mortain and the warrior-bishop Odo of Bayeux. Then came the great barons, men whose names were destined to be heard often in later English history: William of Warenne, Roger of Montgomery, Ralph of Tosny, Robert of Eu, Richard of Evreux. The wily priest Lanfranc was there, and Maurilius, Archbishop of Rouen, and Geoffrey, Bishop of Coutances.

To these men William presented his case for the invasion of England.

He spoke first of all of Harold's oath, which many of them had witnessed. He told them of the pope's backing and showed them the sacred emblems Alexander II had sent him.

He pointed out, also, that the time was as ripe for an

attack on England as it would ever be. Normandy's traditional enemies in France were at their weakest. Anjou was divided by a bitter civil war between the two nephews of Count Geoffrey the Hammer. France itself was ruled by a boy-king, Philip I, whose guardians were friendly to William. This was the time to strike!

The great assembly of Normans, held at Lillebonne, debated the idea hotly. William withdrew from the hall to let them consider his plan without him.

Many of the barons were opposed. Though they were the great-great-grandchildren of Rolf's Vikings, they had lost the taste for naval warfare. They drew back from the kind of sea invasion that was necessary. Harold, they said, was an able warrior, and he commanded a fleet of skilled sailors, including many fierce Danes whose fathers had come to England in the service of Cnut.

Then, too, Normandy was at peace now after three decades of costly war. Why return to battle? Why not be content? They had conquered much of Anjou, and all of Brittany and Maine. It was time to settle down, to pay for those old wars rather than start a new one. England was large and populous, Normandy small. It was foolhardy to start such an enterprise.

While the Normans thus debated, a voice rose above all the others. It was that of William Fitz-Osbern, Duke William's companion, and son of that Osbern who was slain while guarding the young duke more than thirty years before.

"Why dispute ye thus?" William Fitz-Osbern bellowed. "He is your lord and he has need of you. It were rather your duty to make your offers now, and not to await his request. If you fail him now, and he gain his ends, by God he will remember it. Prove you love him and act accordingly."

The barons were still reluctant. They agreed to help William, but only to a limited extent. When the duke returned to the hall, the barons sent Fitz-Osbern up to tell him of their decision.

Carried away by his enthusiasm, Fitz-Osbern boldly told the duke that all present would support him, and that those who in the past had given him the service of two mounted knights would now provide him with four.

At this an outcry arose. A baron pointed at Fitz-Osbern and shouted, "We did not charge you to make such an answer to the duke. Within the duke's own lands we will serve him as is due, but we are not bound to aid him to conquer another man's kingdom. Besides, if we once render him double service, and follow him across the sea, he will make it a right and custom for the future. He will burden our children with the obligation. It shall not be!"

Confusion prevailed. Faced with this opposition from his own barons, William ended the meeting. Shrewdly he adopted a different tactic. He sent for the barons, one by one, and asked each in turn to pledge support for the invasion.

No baron face to face with the duke was courageous enough to defy him. Although many felt, in the words of Duke William's chronicler William of Poitiers, that "the enterprise [was] too difficult, far beyond the strength of Normandy," each baron now offered to join the invasion. Robert of Mortain promised to provide 120 ships manned with fighting men; his brother, Bishop Odo of Bayeux, a hundred ships. William of Evreux offered eighty ships, William Fitz-Osbern and Robert of Eu sixty apiece. The other barons made similar pledges.

All Normandy stirred with excitement. The common people, told that the pope himself had blessed the invasion,

did their best to help, contributing farm produce and merchandise and labor to aid the campaign. Nor did William seek only in Normandy for support. He let it be known that any warrior in Christendom was welcome to join him. What had begun as William's private campaign of conquest was turning into a kind of holy crusade against the usurper Harold.

The forces gathered. Adventurers flocked to William's standard from all over Europe, attracted by talk of good pay and the promise of land in conquered England. They came from Burgundy and Aquitaine, from Maine and Anjou, from the German states, from Flanders, from the Norman colonies in southern Italy. Some were wealthy nobles looking for adventure, others were landless men-at-arms hoping to win fortune and land in William's service.

Spring yielded to summer. The seaports of Normandy

Building and launching the fleet

rang with the sounds of hammers as an army of carpenters turned the fine oak trees of William's domain into ships to bring men to England.

Fully aware of all that was taking place, and ready to face the worst that Duke William could offer, King Harold of England waited in readiness.

HAROLD'S MILITARY STRENGTH was considerable, but it was poorly organized. On the day he took the throne England did not even have a navy of its own. There was simply an understanding that in time of war the king had the power to requisition private ships and civilian sailors for the country's defense. It was a large force on which he could draw, but it took time to bring it together, and there was resistance from those who did not care to serve.

The land forces were similarly scattered. The only permanent soldiers were the king's private bodyguard, a band of well-trained professional soldiers known by the Danish term, *housecarles*. They were ready to fight at any time.

The bulk of the army was contained in the *fyrd*, or local militia. The men of the fyrd were the wealthier minor lords, known as *thegns*, who were required to do military service when asked by the king. In case of war the housecarles would become the "officers" of this loosely organized and untrained militia. Finally came the peasants, who also had to serve in time of war. They had no military training at all and, unlike the men of the fyrd, did not even have real weapons, but had to fight with clubs or with stones tied on sticks.

Harold knew that he could call together a vast army and a powerful navy, far greater than anything William could muster. But most of Harold's warriors were farmers or small landlords, who were not eager to lay down their lives in battle, and who impatiently insisted on going home even when the enemy threatened to attack. In a pitched battle Harold's hordes might be of little avail against a smaller but far fiercer body of William's professional soldiers. This had been the curse of English kings for centuries. Even Alfred the Great, fighting desperately to keep his country from the Danish heel in the ninth century, had nearly failed because his soldiers deserted at harvest time each year to return to their fields.

With invasions from Normandy and from Norway both being planned, Harold realized he had to keep England in a state of military readiness. Tostig's invasion in May had been only a foretaste of what awaited. And so—while in

Normandy William's men felled trees, fashioned them into ships, and hauled them on pulleys down to the sea—King Harold called out the militia early in summer.

He mobilized all England. He stationed the men of the fyrd all along the southern coast of England, facing Normandy. He assembled a large fleet off the Isle of Wight and took personal command. Through May and June, July and August, King Harold and his warriors patrolled England's southern coast, ready to repel invaders.

But no invaders came.

The summer dragged along in idleness. Day after day the fair-haired king scanned the horizon. His spies had told him that William had been busy for months, gathering strength for the invasion. But now it was nearly September. The fighting season soon would be over. Where was William? Why did the invasion not commence?

Harold's army and navy began to grumble. Summer was ending. The wheat stood golden on the stalk. Time had come to begin the task of harvesting. All summer, women had done the work of men on the farms of England while their men had waited uselessly for an invasion that seemed only a cruel hoax. The king did not have the right to keep the fyrd mobilized indefinitely.

Tension grew in Harold's army. Tempers ran high. The king ran the risk of provoking a mutiny. Provisions were dwindling, and the harvest work beckoned.

On September 8 Harold bowed to the inevitable. He had kept his forces in readiness for four months, in vain. Now he had to let them go. The fyrd was disbanded. Thousands of relieved soldiers began to straggle toward their homes throughout England. As for Harold's fleet, he kept it together as best he could, ordering it to London so that it could be ready to defend the country on short notice. Many of the ships were lost on the voyage, though.

So by mid-September England lay open to attack. No militia, no fleet stood guard along the southern shores. Harold, like all the Old English kings before him, had bucked against Saxon independent-mindedness. He could not compel his militia to serve him all year.

England lay open. And attack came.

But not from Normandy.

INVASION!

After almost twenty years, Harold Hardrada of Norway had come to claim the crown of England.

The old Norse saga relates:

> The host of Harold Hardrada gathered in Solundir. When he was ready to leave he first went to the shrine of St. Olaf, opened it, and cut his hair and nails; then he shut the shrine and threw the keys out onto the River Nid, and went southward with his host. So many men had gathered to him that it is said he had nearly 240 ships, besides store-ships and small vessels.

A vast armada came down out of Norway, swept along by a favoring north wind. Harold Hardrada was traveling as though he meant to stay in England a while. This was no mere raiding expedition. The Norwegian king had brought with him his Russian-born wife, Queen Elizabeth, and Olaf, one of his two sons. Aboard his ship there rode the giant king's full wardrobe, all his shining armor and gleaming swords, his household goods, his helmets with their Viking wings. He had brought his banner, called the Land-Waster, bearing the image of a fierce black raven. Never had the Land-Waster been unfurled in a losing battle.

Most spectacularly, Harold Hardrada carried with him to England his entire royal treasure. In his long and successful career of warfare the great Norwegian had amassed much gold, which he had caused to be melted down into one enormous ingot, so heavy it took a dozen men to lift it on board. This giant ingot of pure gold accompanied Harold Hardrada to England.

The Norse saga tells us how his fleet gathered strength as it traveled:

> When King Harold Hardrada was ready for the expedition to England and a fair wind rose, he sailed out to sea with all his fleet; he reached Shetland, and lay a short while there, and then sailed southward to the Orkneys, whence he took many men, and the earls Paul and Erlend, the sons of Thorfinn the earl. He left there Queen Elizabeth and his daughters Maria and Ingigerd. Then he sailed southward past Scotland till he came off England.

Supporters flocked to his banner. Tostig met the Norsemen in Scotland, at the River Tyne, with a force of men that he had been assembling all summer. Tostig's ally, King Malcolm of Scotland, added reinforcements. From Ireland came warriors of Viking descent. Godred of Iceland, a famous sea raider, joined the invading force with his valiant men.

Harold Hardrada stopped first at the town of Cleveland, on the Yorkshire coast. The saga observes that:

> He went ashore, and ravaged and subdued the land, meeting no resistance. Thereupon he sailed to Scarborough and fought against the townsmen; he went up on a high rock near the town, and set fire to a large pile of logs which he made. The Norwegians took large poles and lifted it up and threw it down into the town. Soon one house after the other began to burn, and the whole town was destroyed. The Norsemen slew many people, and took all the property they could get. There was no other choice for the English who wanted to save their lives but to ask peace and become King Harold Hardrada's men; thus he subdued the land wherever he went.

There were few English ships in northern waters, and the sudden fury of Harold Hardrada's attack caught the English by surprise. They could only flee. In mid-September the invaders reached the town of Riccall on the River Ouse, less than ten miles from the city of York. There they camped.

York had been Tostig's capital when he was Earl of Northumbria. Now Earl Morcar ruled there. Tostig and Harold Hardrada assembled their men at Riccall and prepared to attack York.

By this time word had reached King Harold in London that the Norsemen had invaded his kingdom. At once Harold sent word to his recently disbanded militia that all men must return to service at once. Assembling as many soldiers as he could on such short notice, Harold set out at once to go to the defense of York.

York is almost two hundred miles northwest of London, and Harold's army traveled on foot. It would take days for the English king to reach York. The burden of defense fell upon the forces of Earls Edwin and Morcar.

Harold Hardrada left a force at Riccall to guard his brightly painted ships, which thronged the Ouse from bank to bank. With the rest of his troops he marched on York. It was September 20, 1066.

The army of Harold Hardrada and Tostig met the army of Edwin and Morcar at a place called Gate Fulford, situated on the Ouse two miles south of York itself. The men of York fought desperately to keep the Norsemen from gaining entrance to their city. All day long the battle raged. This is what the Norse poem called the *Fornmanna Sogur* says:

> When the host of the earls came down, Harold Hardrada went ashore and began to array his men: one wing stood on the river bank, and the other higher up, near a ditch which was deep, broad, and full of water. The earls let their arrays go down along the river, and most of their men; the standard of Harold Hardrada was near the river; there the ranks were thick; but they were thinnest at the ditch, and least to be depended upon.
>
> Thither Morcar came down with his standard. The wing of the Norsemen by the ditch retreated, and the English followed them, thinking they were going to flee; but when Harold Hardrada saw that his men retired along the ditch, he ordered a war blast to be blown, and urged them on. He had the standard Land-Waster carried forward, and made so hard an attack that all were driven back. There was great slaughter in the English host. When the king hardened the attack,

the earl and his men fled along the river upward; only those who followed him escaped, but so many had fallen that large streams of blood in many places flowed over the plains. The English fell by hundreds. Many jumped into the ditch, and the slain lay there so thick that the Norsemen walked across it with dry feet on human bodies. . . .

The battle of Gate Fulford shattered the army of Edwin and Morcar. The earls fell back. Their role in the next few days is unclear. We know that the people of York, with the invaders at their gates, made peace with Harold Hardrada and agreed to help him in his conquest of southern England. Did Morcar and Edwin join in this agreement? Did they agree to betray Harold to the Norwegian invader? The record is silent.

Someone—either Morcar and Edwin, or else the townspeople of York—surrendered the city to Harold Hardrada. It was agreed that the Northumbrians would give Harold Hardrada hostages against their obedience.

Now the Norwegian king made a fatal mistake. He did not move his headquarters to York. York was a walled city, ideally suited for defense. But Harold Hardrada mysteriously failed to take possession of York. Instead, he withdrew to his earlier position at Riccall. There the final negotiations with the men of York were completed. Then Harold Hardrada left his son Olaf in charge of the Riccall camp and took most of his forces off to another part of Yorkshire to await the delivery of the English hostages.

The new place of encampment for the invading host was Stamford Bridge, twelve miles from Riccall. It had once been the home of the ancient Northumbrian kings. Perhaps Harold Hardrada's pride, or his sense of history, led him to pitch his camp there. It was not a wise choice strategically. The River Derwent ran through the village. It was wide, flat country, hard to defend in a military encounter. All the eastern roads of Yorkshire converged there.

For whatever reason, Harold Hardrada drew up his camp at Stamford Bridge on the evening of September 24. His men were tired. Four days earlier they had fought a bitter battle with the Yorkshiremen. Then they had marched back to Riccall, and finally another dozen miles on to Stamford Bridge. Harold Hardrada intended to give his men several days of rest before they resumed their path of conquest.

There was no rest to be had, though. As the morning sun rose on September 25, a surprise awaited the weary Norsemen.

A cloud of dust appeared on the road from York.

Harold of England was arriving, with an army to challenge the invaders!

THE NORSEMEN WERE TAKEN ABACK. They had expected King Harold of England to arrive eventually, of course. But no one had dreamed that he could cover the distance from London to York in so short a time.

King Harold had carried out one of the greatest marches in history. Driving his men along with constant vigor, he had averaged nearly fifty miles a day on foot, reaching York from London in an unheard-of four days! Coming up from the south, the English soldiers had reached the town of Tadcaster, nine miles from York, late on September 24. Halting there for the night, they had marched into the unguarded city of York the next day. The Yorkshiremen had told King Harold where Harold Hardrada and his forces were encamped. Quickly the English king had his men on the road again, marching toward Stamford Bridge and the long-awaited clash between Harold of England and Harold of Norway.

It was a fiercely hot day. Harold's fighting men sweated as they stolidly marched toward the unsuspecting Vikings. In the vanguard of King Harold's forces were the housecarles, the trained bodyguards, waving aloft Harold's personal flag, the Standard of the Fighting Man. Behind them came the militiamen, the fyrd. All marched at a steady clip, roaring battle songs in the harsh Anglo-Saxon English. They carried battle-axes on their shoulders, shields on their arms. They wore knee-length tunics, gray now with the dust of the road. Their legs were bare, their feet shod in leather. It was an army of fair-haired men, stocky and strong, and the bright morning sunlight glinted off their helmets, tipped with hornlike points.

The startled Norsemen scrambled into fighting positions. As Harold Hardrada bellowed commands the Vikings formed themselves into a tight half circle, interlocking their shields to form an impenetrable wall. Because of the hot weather the overconfident Norsemen had left their coats of mail behind at Riccall. They had brought with them to Stamford Bridge only their helmets and shields, their swords and their spears.

King Harold Hardrada inspected his men and gave his orders. "Those who stand outermost in the array," he boomed, "shall put the handles of their spears down on the ground, and the points against the breasts of the English if they advance. Let us stand firm and take care not to break this array."

As he rode out on his huge black horse to view his troops,

Harold Hardrada's steed stumbled beneath the huge Viking's weight. Harold Hardrada was thrown to the ground, and his massive body landed hard. But he came swiftly to his feet, and said, "A fall bodes a lucky journey."

In the English force, King Harold turned to a warrior at his side and asked, "Do you know the tall man who fell from his horse?"

"It is the king of the Norsemen."

"He is a tall and noble-looking man," King Harold of England observed. "But I think his luck has left him."

The English king was eager to avoid a battle if he could. Every man lost today was one less who could help to defend England against that other menace, the Norman duke. So, while Harold Hardrada waited, a grim and terrible figure with his curling locks streaming from his helmet, with his huge sword aloft, his shield shining in the blazing sun, his Land-Waster standard flying aloft, King Harold of England sent forth heralds to talk of peace.

"Where is Tostig the son of Godwin?" the heralds asked.

"I am here," Tostig answered, stepping forward with his battle-ax over his shoulder.

The English envoy said, "Harold thy brother sends thee greeting, and offers thee peace and friendship."

"What terms," Tostig asked, "does the king offer me if I should lay down my weapons and crave peace?"

"A brother's love," was the reply. "And the fair earldom of Northumberland. A third of Harold's kingdom shall be thine to rule."

"And if I accept these terms," Tostig said, "what shall be given to my ally, Harold the King of Norway?"

The envoy's reply was scornful. "Seven feet of English ground will King Harold grant the Norseman. Or perhaps, since he is said to be a giant, twelve inches more."

"Go then," said Tostig, "and tell my brother, King Harold, to prepare for battle. It shall not be said among Norsemen that Earl Tostig brought Harold, King of Norway, to England and then deserted him in the midst of his foes."

The heralds returned to the English lines. Two weary armies confronted one another—the Norsemen, still showing the effects of the battle of Gate Fulford five days before; the English, fatigued by their desperate march from London.

The battle began.

The English charged, King Harold leading the way with his battle-ax upraised. The attackers crashed against the Norwegian shield-wall and hewed away with mace and sword and ax. The Norsemen stood firm, yielding not an inch. In their midst the mightiest of all was the giant Harold Hardrada, nearly seven feet tall, swinging with two hands the long sword that few other men could even lift. His eyes blazed with the joy of battle, and from his throat burst the wild war-songs of his Viking forefathers, and about him grew a heap of English dead.

Harold of England, finding his men thrown back by the immovable Norse shield-wall, tried a clever trick. He gave the order to retreat. The Englishmen began to flee. Harold Hardrada's army, seeing the enemy in apparent disarray, gave a great shout and followed after.

The ruse worked. Harold had fooled the Norsemen into breaking their shield-wall. As Harold Hardrada's warriors fell out of formation, the "fleeing" Englishmen suddenly halted, ending their feigned retreat, and turned to renew the battle with greater vigor than before, breaking through the Norwegian lines.

This is the account of the conflict in the Norse saga:

> When Harold Hardrada saw that his men were falling, he rushed into the fray where it was hottest. Many men fell on both sides. Harold, King of Norway, fought with the greatest bravery, and became so eager and furious that he rushed forward out of the array, dealing blows on all sides. Neither helmet nor coat of mail could withstand him. He went through the ranks of his foes as if he were walking through air, for all who came near him fell back.
>
> Then, as the English almost fled, Harold Hardrada was hit with an arrow in the throat, so that a stream of blood gushed from his mouth. This was his deathwound. He fell there with all the men who had gone forward around him, except those who retreated and kept their standard.

Harold Hardrada had died a Viking's death, but the battle still boiled. Tostig still lived, and he seized Harold Hardrada's standard and urged the Norsemen on.

There was a halt in the battle. Harold took advantage of it to send envoys once more to Tostig, offering him his old earldom of Northumbria if he would cease to fight. Tostig spurned the envoy. The battle resumed.

With Harold Hardrada dead, the Norsemen were in disarray, and the English were able to break the Viking shield-wall again and again. Dozens of Norsemen fell, and Tostig himself went down to death. As Tostig fell, Norse reinforcements arrived, men from Riccall led by a warrior called Eystein Orri. These fresh soldiers were in full armor, and they plunged immediately into the fray, Eystein Orri seizing the Norse banner. The great heat weakened the mail-clad newcomers, who were already tired because they had virtually run all the way from Riccall to come to Harold Hardrada's aid. Many died of sheer exhaustion. Others peeled off their coats of mail and were slain by English spears. When night descended, the surviving Norsemen slipped away, and King Harold of England held the battlefield in triumph.

Harold Hardrada's son Olaf waited at Riccall. King Harold sent word to him, offering a truce. If Olaf would agree to swear never to invade England again, Harold would let him depart in peace. Olaf readily accepted. Of all Harold Hardrada's hundreds of ships, only twenty-four made the mournful voyage back to Norway. Of every ten men who had sailed with Harold Hardrada, nine had lost their lives on English soil. And Harold Hardrada himself had won nothing but a grave—the "seven feet of English ground" that Harold of England had mockingly promised him.

Harold returned to York. There he buried his tempestuous brother Tostig, and feasted his men for their victory. There, too, he probably sent for the brother Earls Edwin and Morcar to ask them some disturbing questions. Why had they yielded so willingly to Harold Hardrada after the battle of Gate Fulford? Why had they not aided at all in the battle of Stamford Bridge? Were they loyal or were they not?

We do not know what answers Edwin and Morcar made. Perhaps they simply excused themselves by saying they had suffered heavily at Gate Fulford and had not had strength for further combat. Harold soon had other worries and turned his attention away from the northern earls.

He was still at York in the early days of October when a messenger stumbled into town, breathless and exhausted, bearing the news that King Harold had feared since that day nine months before when first he donned King Edward's crown.

The Normans had landed!

Duke William's troops had come ashore in southern England, at nine in the morning on Thursday, September 28.

King Harold, who had just completed a man-killing march of 190 miles from London to York, and who had just fought a grueling, desperate battle against foreign invaders, now had to do it all over again. After only a few days of rest, he was faced with the urgent need to march southward and confront his Norman foe.

IT HAD BEEN A LONG, FRUSTRATING SUMMER for William of Normandy.

First of all had come the task, easily enough accomplished, of winning the pope's blessing for his invasion of England. Then had come the harder job of gaining the support of the Norman barons. Next, William had had to assemble his forces and build his fleet.

All that had been done methodically and smoothly enough. The vessels were built and dragged to the sea, and laden with cargoes of provisions—meat and wine, javelins and bows. Knights in armor with their horses and equipment had come to the ports to board the ships.

It was a great fleet, but just how great is a matter of some question. One of the old chronicles says that William had 50,000 knights and 10,000 soldiers of lesser rank. If that is true, it would have been the largest army ever assembled in Europe up to that time. But the figures are certainly exaggerated. The Norman writers probably wanted to boast of Normandy's might, while the Saxon writers were able to excuse England's defeat by claiming that William brought an enormous host.

William's army probably numbered between 5,000 and 10,000. Of these, two to three thousand may have been cavalry, the rest archers and foot soldiers. Even that was an invading force of tremendous size, and the transportation problems must have been immense, when one considers that thousands of horses had to be brought across the English Channel as well as provisions for men and horses.

The twelfth-century Norman poet Robert Wace, whose epic, the *Roman de Rou*, is the best surviving early account of the Norman invasion, says that William had exactly 696 ships. This may have been correct, but included only the large vessels. A later French historian, La Roncière, wrote that William had "696 large vessels, followed by boats and wherries which brought the total to three thousand craft of all kinds."

We know what these ships looked like because they are depicted for us in the famous Bayeux Tapestry, which William's half-brother Bishop Odo caused to be woven about twenty years later. The Bayeux Tapestry portrays all the events of the contest between William and Harold, from the moment Harold set out on his ill-fated European journey in 1064 onward to the bloody climax. The tapestry shows the Norman ships as long and low, Viking style, with high, curving prows carved with the features of dragons or leopards. A single mast rose amidships, bearing one brightly striped sail. The hulls of the ships themselves are shown as gaily painted in red and blue stripes.

Early in August, William ordered this great fleet to assemble at the Norman port of Dives, at the mouth of the river of that name. The painted ships rode at anchor while unfavorable winds blew. William could only wait for the wind to change before setting out for England. Across the

Channel, Harold of England waited also, his fleet and army ready to defend England's shores.

William of Poitiers set down this account of William at Dives:

> Having forbidden any kind of pillage, the duke nourished at his own expense 50,000 knights during the month that contrary winds detained them at the mouth of the Dives, so great was his moderation and prudence. He provided abundantly for the needs of the knights and the foreigners, but did not permit anything to be taken from anybody whatsoever. The cattle and the flocks of the inhabitants of the country grazed in the fields with as much security as if they had been in a sanctified place. The harvests waited intact for the sickle of the reaper, having been neither trampled down in the arrogance of the knights nor plundered by the forager. The weak or unarmed man went as he would, singing on his horse, and he saw the men in arms and was not afraid.

While the contrary northeast wind cooped the Normans up at Dives, William stewed in thwarted eagerness to be off. His army grew restless. It seemed that the elements themselves were against the enterprise.

The truth was quite the opposite: the winds that held William back were his best friends, though he could not have known it then. For while his men grew restless, Harold's men were growing even more uneasy. Where William ruled by sheer will, Harold was bound by the traditions of England. The time came when Harold could no longer keep his men in arms. The guardians who had waited all summer for William were set free at last, and returned to their homes.

Harold began to disband his militia about September 8. Unaware of this, and prepared to meet opposition, William decided to set out for England on September 12.

The wind had changed, but not very usefully. William needed a south wind; instead, he got a wind from the north and west, the same wind that was wafting Harold Hardrada's fleet toward northern England. Nevertheless, William gave the orders to sail. The fleet moved eastward along the Norman coast, as far as the port of St. Valéry, at the mouth of the Somme.

Here the Normans dropped anchor again, for the weather had again turned foul. A western gale smashed into the Norman fleet. Dozens of ships foundered, and the bodies of dead Norman warriors were washed up on the shore. William ordered these corpses to be buried secretly, at night, for the sake of his army's morale. Even so, his men grew troubled. "The man is mad who seeks to seize the land of another," they muttered. "God is offended by such designs, and to prove it, He refuses us a favorable wind."

After gales came rain. The Normans huddled in their muddied tents, cursing the chill weather. William tried to make his men happy with extra rations of wine and meat. Still they murmured bitterly and talked of going home.

A miracle was needed. William produced one. He sent for the abbot of the monastery of St. Valéry and ordered the priest to exhume the body of the patron saint of the town. St. Valéry had worked miracles before. Now his body was paraded in solemn procession before Duke William's host while every man prayed for a change of wind. That very night the prayers were granted. The wind, which had been blowing steadily from the west, veered to southerly. The gales died down. The sun glowed in golden splendor on the morning of September 27.

A second time William had been befriended by the wind and the rain. If he had sailed in August, as he originally intended, the Norman fleet would have been met by the full force of Harold's defenders. But the winds held Duke William in port at Dives, and while William waited, Harold's forces collapsed. Then, William tried again on September 12, but was driven back into St. Valéry. If he had succeeded in crossing to England that day, Harold might have reassembled his militia in time to put up a strong fight.

As it happened, though, the gale delayed William two weeks more, until September 27. And by that time, as we have seen, the ranks of England's soldiers had been thinned by the battle with Hardrada, and king and army were weary. The situation was made to order for William.

He knew none of these things on the morning of September 27. Duke William simply hoped God would favor him on the hazardous journey across the English Channel.

The Norman fleet sails for England

The Normans set sail at nightfall. William himself led the way in his flagship, about which the poet Wace writes:

> It was called the *Mora*, and was the gift of his duchess, Matilda. On the head of the ship in the front, which mariners call the prow, there was a brazen child bearing an arrow with a bended bow. His face was turned toward England, and thither he looked, as though he was about to shoot.

A lantern slung from the mast of the *Mora* was supposed to guide the other Norman ships. William's vessel was by far the fastest of the fleet, however, and in the darkness it soon left the others behind. When dawn broke, Duke William found himself alone in mid-Channel. Not one of his hundreds of ships was in sight. Had they all perished silently in the darkness? Had Harold's fleet swept down upon them and cut them to pieces, letting William alone sail on unharmed?

The puzzled duke sent a sailor up the mast to spy. "I see only the sky and the sea," the man reported.

William sent for food and drink, and tried to hide his fears. When he had breakfasted, he ordered the seaman to climb the mast again. This time the news was better.

"I see four ships coming," the sailor cried.

Rejoicing, William sent the man up again. And now there was no doubt that the mighty fleet had safely crossed the Channel. "I see a forest of masts and sails!" came the word from the look-out.

No English ships were encountered the whole while. Wace tells us, "The breeze became soft and sweet, and the sea was smooth for their landing." William had made the crossing unchallenged, and now he disembarked without drawing opposition from the English. It struck him as strange. Where was Harold? Where was the English army? Where the English ships? Was this some kind of trap?

William gave the orders for landing. It was nine in the morning, on the twenty-eighth of September, and the Normans were near the bay of Pevensey, on England's southern coast. The invasion host came ashore, just as nearly nine hundred years later, on the sixth of June, 1944, other invaders would reverse the tale and cross from England to land on the beaches of Normandy.

Wace writes of the Norman ships at the beach:

> Each ranged by the other's side. There you might see the good sailors, the sergeants and squires sally forth and unload the ships; cast the anchors, haul the ropes, bear out shields and saddles, and land the warhorses and palfreys.

The archers came forth, and touched land the first, each with his bow strung, and with his quiver full of arrows, slung at his side. All were shaven and shorn; and all clad in short garments, ready to attack, to shoot, to wheel about and skirmish. All stood well equipped, and of good courage for the fight; and they scoured the whole shore, but found not an armed man there.

After the archers had thus gone forth, the knights landed all armed, with their hauberks on, their shields slung at their necks, and their helmets laced. They formed together on the shore, each armed, and mounted on his war-horse. All had their swords girded on, and rode forward into the country with their lances raised.

Not all who came ashore were warriors, though. William had brought men who worked with their hands—carpenters and stonemasons. For one of the most important features of Norman warfare was the use of the fortified castle. From their earliest days the Normans had cemented each victory by building a castle Each castle was built on a mound of earth or on a high, easily defended peak. It was surrounded by an outer stockade, and within the stockade was a water-filled moat. A drawbridge that could be raised in case of attack provided the only entry to the castle. Within were quartered soldiers and their horses. By building castles the Normans could control conquered territory with ease. A small garrison defending the castle could be used to hold a large area in check.

So the castle builders came ashore. In Wace's words:

> Then the carpenters landed, who had great axes in their hands, and planes and adzes hung at their sides.

They took counsel together, and sought for a good place on which to place a castle. They had brought with them, in the fleet, three wooden castles from Normandy, in pieces, all ready for framing together, and they took the materials of one of these out of the ships, all shaped and pierced to receive the pins which they had brought cut and ready in large barrels. And before evening had set in, they had finished a good fort on the English ground, and there they placed their stores. All then ate and drank enough, and were right glad that they were ashore.

One of the last to leave the ships was Duke William himself. His coming ashore was marked with an omen. As he set foot on English soil, in his anxiety and nervousness he stumbled and fell headlong.

"An evil sign!" his men cried.

The quick-witted Duke William had a different interpretation of the omen. He rose to his feet, clutching a handful of sand from the beach.

"See, my lords!" he shouted. "By the splendor of God! I have taken possession of England with both my hands. It is now mine. And what is mine is yours!"

VI

THE BATTLE OF HASTINGS

THE MOST HAZARDOUS PART OF DUKE William's adventure was already over. He had safely made the sixty-mile sea voyage from St. Valéry to the Sussex coast. Not since the Angles, the Saxons, and the Jutes had invaded Britain in the fifth century had anyone succeeded in attacking the island by crossing the Channel. Never again in history has an enemy of England landed an army on the southern coast.

The odds had been against William. His ships were small, and his men were less experienced in naval warfare than Harold's. If the English fleet had been ready and waiting, quite likely the Normans would have been sent to the bottom of the Channel before a man set foot in Sussex.

The English had *not* been waiting. The fleet had been disbanded for three weeks. King Harold himself was up in York on the day William landed, resting after his valiant triumph over the Norwegians at Stamford Bridge.

Duke William had no inkling of the events that had taken place near York. And so he moved cautiously at first. On the day of landing, the Normans occupied themselves by digging in at Pevensey, fortifying themselves on the site of an old Roman encampment.

It was quickly apparent that Pevensey was not an ideal place to use as a headquarters. It was surrounded on the east and north by swampy marshes. The next day the duke sent out scouts, who reported that nearby Hastings would afford a much sounder position strategically.

The Normans moved camp and fleet to Hastings. There they put up another castle of earth and timber and hatched the plans for the invasion. Scouts went out again. They reported that no English army was in sight. Normans went on a foraging expedition in Hastings, seizing all the clothing and provisions they could find. "The English," Wace writes, "were to be seen fleeing before them, driving off their cattle and quitting their houses. Many took shelter in burying places, and even there they were in grievous alarm."

One party of Normans, though, came ashore at the town of Romney and met with resistance. The townspeople fiercely attacked the invaders and killed some of them—the first Norman blood shed in the invasion.

Within a few days news filtered into the Norman camp that Harold Hardrada had invaded England also, and that Harold the English king had gone north to meet him. The outcome of that meeting was not yet known in southern England, although the battle had been over for a week. Duke William was pleased by the news of the rival invasion. Harold of England and Harold of Norway would exhaust one another in their battle, William knew. If luck were really with him, both rulers would be killed in the fray,

The Normans burn Hastings

leaving William with a clear grasp of the English throne. Even if one of the Harolds should survive, his army would be greatly weakened by the battle.

Until he knew more, William had to be cautious. It was no time for rashness. He remained close to his ships, ready for a quick retreat if events turned against him. He concentrated on digging in at Hastings, fortifying his position there.

King Harold, in York, learned of the Norman landing within a few days. His reaction was swift. Ordering an end to the post-battle holiday his men had been taking, he rushed out of York and began to march southward, doubling back along the path he had covered with such furious speed only the week before.

He left York on October second, and by the sixth or seventh he was in London. There he stayed for three or four days while soldiers joined him from the outlying provinces of England. Impatient, eager to be at William's throat at last, Harold could not wait for his whole army to assemble. It took days for messengers to ride out to distant shires with the news, and days more for the fyrd to assemble and come to London.

Harold could not wait.

On October 11 he left London. Only part of his army had joined him. He had his loyal housecarles, though they were wearied from long marching, and their numbers had been sorely thinned at Stamford Bridge. He had the militiamen of Wessex and Sussex. But there were no soldiers from the extreme west of England or from the north. The men of Earls Morcar and Edwin had not yet recovered from their losses at Gate Fulford. They were unable to come to Harold's aid now.

Yet Harold marched without them.

In two days Harold's army had come south to the outskirts of the great forest known as the Andredsweald. Ahead of them lay the coastal plain that William was ravaging. William himself was encamped at Hastings, only fifty miles from King Harold's position on the night of October 13. It had been a busy fortnight for Harold. He had made the round trip from London to York and back again, and now had marched south to the Andredsweald.

He had about 7,000 men at his command, but they were not all of equal value. They included everyone who could be pressed into service on such short notice, and they ranged in ability from skilled housecarles to half-armed peasants with no notion of military discipline.

Harold's own advisers warned the king he was acting too hastily. They told him to wait and gather his full strength before launching an attack on Duke William's grim army of professional soldiers. Why attack at all, they asked? Why not simply form a huge defensive force and lay waste to all the country between London and Hastings? That way, William, penned up along the coast, would be starved out. Unable to advance past the defenders, unable to live off the wasted land, William eventually would have to give up and return to Normandy. Soldiers must be fed, after all.

Harold would have none of it. He had lived in the shadow of William of Normandy for more than a decade; now he could play a waiting game no longer. He yearned to come to grips with the Norman duke. As for laying waste to English farms simply to starve William out, Harold refused. He would not sacrifice the labor of Englishmen that way.

No. He would attack, and drive William and his Normans into the sea. His mind was made up, and no other counsel would he heed.

Duke William too was getting advice—and not always heeding it. He sent scouts northward, who returned to tell him that Harold was "rushing on like a madman." At the same time came a letter to William from Robert FitzWymarc, in London. This FitzWymarc was one of the Frenchmen that Edward the Confessor had brought to England years before. FitzWymarc's father had come from Brittany, and his mother, a Norman, was related to William himself.

Robert FitzWymarc had held the post of Edward the Confessor's *staller*, or chamberlain. He had been one of the four people present at King Edward's death. Now he sent word to William at Hastings that Harold had shattered the forces of Harold Hardrada, the most valient warrior of the northlands, had slain both the Norwegian and his own brother Tostig, and was coming to do the same to Duke William.

"Enheartened by his victory," FitzWymarc wrote, "he comes promptly toward thee, at the head of a strong and innumerable army, against which thine own men will count less than dogs."

The cautious chamberlain warned William against provoking an encounter with King Harold, advising him to remain in his own entrenchments. William would have none of this advice. He told the messenger who had borne him FitzWymarc's letter, "Return to thy master and thank him for his warning, although I had rather it had been more politely worded. I will not take refuge behind my fortifications, and I will fight Harold as soon as possible." And, Duke William added, he would crush any English army that came against him.

On the night of October 13, King Harold halted his troops some seven miles from the Norman lines. He sent some spies who understood French forward to take a measure of Duke William's armed strength.

The spies returned late that night in a state of astonishment. There were, they said "more priests in Willam's camp than there were fighting men in the English army!"

Harold burst out into laughter. He had been in Normandy, of course, and he knew Norman fashion. The spies had seen Norman soldiers with short hair and clean-shaven chins. That was the style of English priests. The mistake was a natural one.

Harold said, "Those whom you have seen in such numbers are not priests, but sturdy soldiers, as they will soon make us feel."

That night both William and Harold laid their plans. By the normal rules of warfare Harold was in a far stronger position. He was defending his home soil, and at least in theory he had the strength of an entire nation on which to draw. William, on the other hand, had only so many men, so much in the way of provisions, and could have no reinforcements. Harold had quickly moved his fleet back into the English Channel to cut off a possible Norman retreat. William was hemmed in along the shore, with Harold's army before him and Harold's fleet behind him.

A wise English king would not have attacked the Normans just then. A wise king would have waited, gathering the full strength of his army, encircling the Normans and keeping them from raiding the land for provisions. Finally, when the Normans began showing signs of hunger, the English could descend and wipe them out in a two-pronged attack.

Harold of Wessex was a wise king. He had governed England well, and he had shown that he understood warfare. This once, though, his wisdom deserted him. Impatience ruled. His overwhelming desire to be rid of William of Normandy once and for all clouded his vision.

To those who came to him and suggested that he lay waste to the farms between his position and William's, Harold replied, "I will not burn houses and villages, neither will I take away the substance of my people." To battle it would be, no sieges, no waiting.

Harold's two younger brothers, Gyrth and Leofwine, saw that the king would not be shaken from this resolve. Gyrth was troubled by the fact that Harold had sworn an oath to

William and had broken it. Gyrth saw that as a sacrilegious act, one that would bring the wrath of God down upon the English side.

"My brother," Gyrth said, "thou canst not deny that either by force or free will thou hast made Duke William an oath on the bodies of the saints. Why then risk thyself in the battle with a perjury upon thee?"

Gyrth suggested that Harold remain behind the lines and allow his brothers to lead the English army. "To us, who have sworn nothing," Gyrth said, "this is a holy and a just war, for we are fighting for our country. Leave us, then, alone to fight this battle, and he who has the right will win."

Harold was obstinate. He replied, "It may be, brother, that it will suit thee better to fight against William than me. But I have not been wont to lie in my room when other men have fought, and William shall not hear that I dare not behold him."

On the evening of October 13 there were negotiations between the two camps. Harold opened them by sending a monk as messenger to William. The messenger was charged to tell the Duke of Normandy that his claim to the English throne was wrongful. True, Harold admitted, King Edward may have promised William the crown many years ago. True, Harold himself had sworn an oath to that effect in 1064. But in the last moments of his life Edward had given the crown to Harold. As William should know, a man's final wishes are binding, no matter what he may have promised earlier. Harold thus was Edward's lawful heir. The witan had so confirmed it by electing Harold king. Therefore, King Harold's messenger concluded, the proper thing for William to do was to withdraw peacefully from England's shores.

William listened to this argument without showing any sign of expression. When he had heard the monk out, he sent a messenger of his own, a monk named Hugues Maigrot, to bear answer to the English king.

Hugues Maigrot came before King Harold and bluntly denied the validity of Harold's whole argument. The monk repeated William's statement that he had come to England justly, that "I was constituted the heir by my lord and kinsman King Edward, in return for the striking honors and numerous benefactions which he, his brother and his followers had received from myself and my barons. He believed me, of all those who were allied to him by birth, the best and most capable, either to aid him while he lived, or to govern his kingdom after his death."

Through the monk, William offered Harold three choices. He could resign his kingdom into William's hands at once. He could submit the dispute to the pope for arbitration. Or, finally, he could let it be decided by a duel of single combat between Harold and William.

Harold found the first choice impossible. As for the second, the pope had already stated his opinion on the case, so arbitration would mean defeat. And, while Harold was no coward and did not shrink from combat, he thought it unwise to stake something as important as the crown of England upon the outcome of a single duel, where a lucky thrust could decide everything. Back went the messengers with Harold's reply:

"I will not resign my title, I will not refer it to the pope, nor will I accept the single combat."

Even this did not end the negotiations. Then as now, a kind of minuet of pre-battle discussions customarily took place before men went to war. William had a reply ready for Harold. He spoke to Hugues Maigrot:

"Go and tell Harold, that if he will keep his former compact with me, I will leave to him all the country which lies north of the River Humber, and will give his brother Gyrth all the lands which their father Godwin held, in Wessex. If he still persist in refusing my offers, then thou shalt tell him, before all his people, that he is a perjurer and a liar; that he, and all who shall support him, are excommunicated by the mouth of the pope; and that the decree to that effect is in my hands."

The chronicler records that Harold and his counselors were very grave as Hugues Maigrot solemnly delivered this message, and that Harold paled when the dread word "excommunicated" was uttered. But his resolve to do battle was unshaken.

To yield now was impossible. Every English thegn, or lord, knew that. William had promised his followers English lands, and what the invaders received, the English must lose. One of Harold's men declared, "We must fight, whatever may be the danger to us. They come, not only to ruin us, but to ruin our descendants also, and take from us the country of our ancestors."

Harold agreed. "We march to battle," he told Duke William's emissary. "May the Lord pronounce between William and me which of us is in the right."

THE CHRONICLER WILLIAM OF MALMESBURY, who was born thirty years after the Battle of Hastings, collected the reports of eyewitnesses and included them in his great work, the *Gesta Regum Anglorum* ("Deeds of the English King"). William of Malmesbury tells us that the two armies spent the night before the battle in very different ways.

"The English, as we have heard," he wrote, "passed the

night without sleep, in drinking and singing." Seven miles away were the Normans, "who passed the whole night in confessing their sins, and received the sacrament in the morning." The two Norman bishops, Odo of Baycux and Geoffrey of Coutances, led the prayers and blessed the weapons of the warriors.

Harold and his army had taken their positions on a hill called Senlac, seven miles northeast of Hastings. The road from Hastings to London ran that way, along the tops of low hills, but at Senlac the ground dipped to form a sloping valley. The hill itself ran from the east to the southwest, with higher ground behind it, covered with thick forest. At the foot of the southern slope of the 260-foot-high hill was the valley, forming an area about a thousand yards across. The western part of this area was marshy.

Harold was thus in a first-rate defensive position. He occupied the high ground, so William's forces would have to charge uphill to do battle. In order to reach the English, the Normans would have to cross the open valley, exposing themselves to easy attack.

The English king planned to fight a defensive battle. He had seen at Stamford Bridge how difficult it was for attackers to break through a wall of shields. He intended to use Harold Hardrada's tactic here. The English would form a solid barrier with their shields. The Normans, mounting the hill, would suffer heavy losses in the fruitless attempt to break the wall. Finally, when the Normans were thinned in number, they could be driven toward the sea.

It was an excellent strategy—so long as the shield-wall held firm.

Early on the morning of the fourteenth, Harold began to arrange his troops. Unlike the Normans, he had neither archers nor cavalry, only foot soldiers. In large measure that fact dictated his strategy. In the center of his line he planted his own battle standard, the Fighting Man, the figure of an armed warrior embroidered in precious gems on cloth of gold. Around the standard he stationed his best men, the housecarles, numbering two or three thousand at most. The rest of the front line consisted of men of the fyrd—thegns and wealthier peasants, who had helmets and shirts of mail, shields and battle-axes. Behind them were arrayed a motley crew of peasants, armed with sticks, with stones, with sickles and scythes.

The Norman troops presented a much more frightening aspect. They were hardened warriors, schooled to battle in the long civil wars of Normandy. The cavalry looked particularly imposing, with the mounted men astride fierce, stamping chargers. The mounted knights wore long coats of ring mail and helmets with steel nosepieces. They carried lances and swords. Then, too, there were the archers and crossbowmen, and the foot soldiers.

At dawn, the Normans had ceased their praying and begun to arm. Duke William tied around his neck (or, as a Norse chronicle has it, to his banner) a bag containing some of the saintly relics on which Harold had sworn his oath. Then he donned his armor. As his attendants gave him his coat of mail they presented it with the hind side front. It might have been interpreted as another omen of defeat, but William was always ready to see the sunny side of any such omen. Laughing, he said, "It means my dukedom shall be turned into a kingdom."

When all was ready, the Normans streamed from their tents and assembled to march. Standing on a hill, Duke William surveyed his men and arrayed them into three divisions. The Normans themselves, led by William,

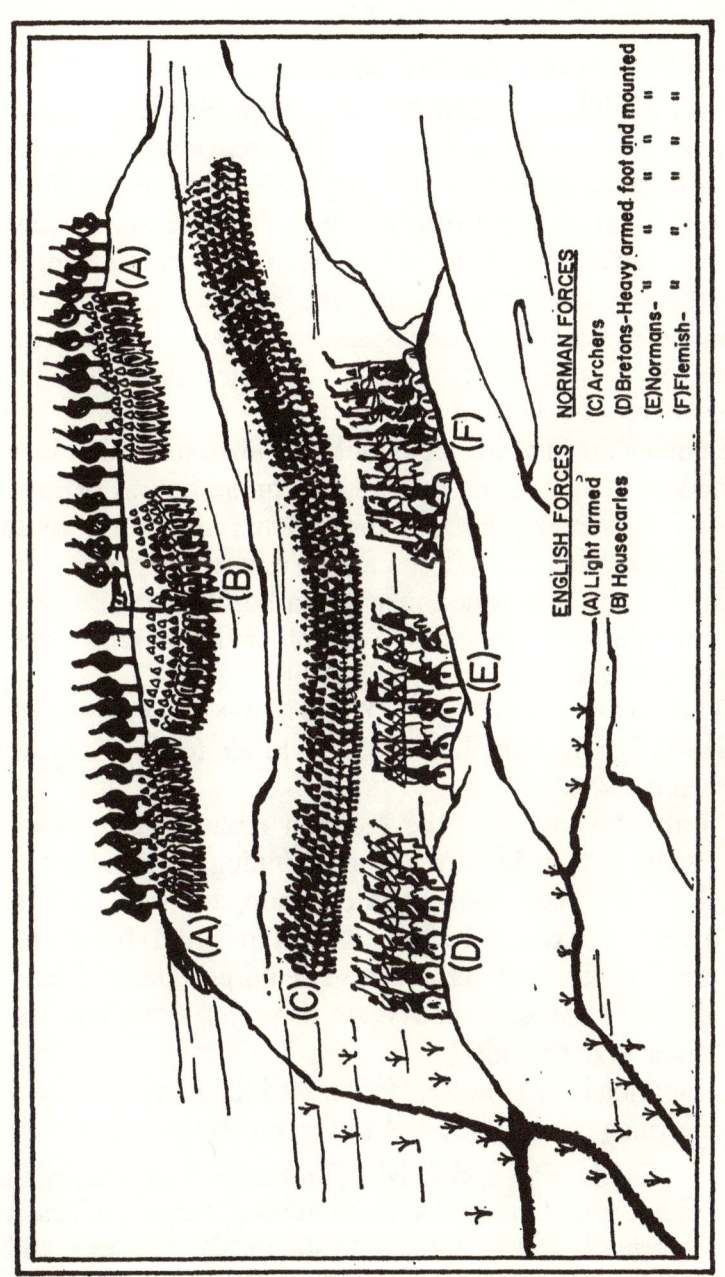

The beginning of the Battle of Hastings. October 14, 1066

formed the center division, which was the strongest. To the left, William placed the men from Brittany, Anjou, Maine, and Poitou. His right wing consisted of soldiers from Flanders and other outlying lands. Each of the three divisions was arranged the same way. In front were placed the archers and the men who wielded the newly invented crossbow. Behind them came the foot soldiers, heavily armored in mail, and carrying spear and shield. In the rear were the dreaded cavalry, mailed knights who had never known defeat in battle.

Looking down at his men, Duke William told them how confident he was of success and how proud he was of their valor. "It is now," he told them, "that your arms must prove your strength and courage. No road is open for retreat. On one side armed men and a hostile and unknown country bar your passage. On the other the sea and other armed men are opposed to your flight."

The soldiers roared back, "You will not see one coward, Duke William! None here will fear to die for love of you, if need be."

"I thank you well," the Norman replied. "For God's sake spare not; strike hard at the beginning; stay not to the spoil. All the booty shall be in common, and there will be plenty for everyone." He warned them to fight to the death, for the English were certain to spare no prisoners. "I have no doubt of the victory. We are come for glory, and the victory is in our hands!"

Mounting his war-horse, William led the procession from the Norman camp. Robert Wace describes the scene:

> The barons, and knights, and men-at-arms were all now armed; the foot soldiers were well equipped, each bearing bow and sword; on their heads were caps, and

to their feet were bound buskins. Some had good hides which they had bound round their bodies; and many were clad in frocks, and had quivers and bows hung to their girdles. The knights had hauberks and swords, boots of steel and shining helmets; shields at their necks, and in their hands lances. And all had their means of identification, so that each might know his fellow, and Norman might not strike Norman, nor Frenchman kill his countryman by mistake.

Those on foot led the way, with serried ranks, bearing their bows. The knights rode next, supporting the archers from behind. Thus both horse and foot kept their course and order of march as they began; in close ranks at a gentle pace, that the one might not pass or separate from the other. All went firmly and compactly, bearing themselves gallantly.

As the Normans approached the enemy lines, scouts returned with the news that the English were on Senlac hill. Before nine in the morning, the Normans had covered the seven miles from their camp to Senlac, and they could see the English on the far side of the valley, occupying the hill.

According to the chronicle of the Anglo-Saxons, the English were taken by surprise when the Normans appeared so early. The actual words of the chronicler, set down in the English language of nine hundred years ago, were, "Wyllelm him com ongean on unwær ær his folc gefylced wære." (William came upon him unexpectedly, before his army was set in order.)

Seeing the Normans approach, King Harold hastily moved his men into their shield-wall formation. Side by side they planted themselves, shields interlocking, battle-axes at the ready.

"The Normans are good fighters," Harold told his troops, "valiant on foot and on horseback, and well used to battle. All is lost if they once penetrate our ranks."

Across the valley now came the Normans in their thousands, an awesome sight. Sunlight flashed from their armor, that Saturday morning in October. High above the Norman ranks fluttered the banner of the pope, as though telling the English that God Himself came to fight against them today.

In Wace's account:

> As soon as the two armies were in full view of each other, great noise and tumult arose. You might hear the sounds of many trumpets, of bugles, and of horns; and then you might see men ranging themselves in line, lifting their shields, raising their lances, bending their bows, handling their arrows, ready for assault and defense.

The Normans ride to Battle

The English stood ready to their post, the Normans still moved on; and when they drew near, the English were to be seen stirring to and fro; were going and coming; troops ranging themselves in order; some with their color rising, others turning pale; some making ready their arms, others raising their shields; the brave man rousing himself to fight, the coward trembling at the approach of danger.

In the midst of the Norman host rode Taillefer, the minstrel, poet to the Norman court, Taillefer "who sang right well, riding mounted on a swift horse, before the Duke, singing of Charlemagne and of Roland, of Olivier and the peers who died in Roncesvalles." In the tense moment just before the start of the battle that would change English history, Taillefer the minstrel approached his master Duke William.

"A boon, sire!" he cried. "I have long served you, and

you owe me for all such service. Today, so please you, you shall repay it. I ask and beseech you earnestly, allow me to strike the first blow in the battle!"

"I grant it," Duke William answered.

So, to the astonishment of the English, a minstrel rode out of the Norman ranks, singing lustily, tossing his sword high in the air and catching it again with a juggler's skill. He spurred his horse to a gallop, up the steep hill toward the English line, and struck an Englishman dead with the first thrust of his lance.

Then he drew his sword and struck another, crying out, "Come on, come on! What do ye, sirs, lay on, lay on!"

An instant later Taillefer disappeared beneath the blows of English battle-axes and was seen alive no more. The battle had been joined!

"Loud and far resounded the bray of the horns," Wace's poem declares. "And the shocks of the lances, the mighty strokes of maces, and the quick clashing of swords. The Normans shouted '*Diex aie!*' and the English people, 'Out! Out!' Then came the cunning maneuvers, the rude shocks and strokes of the lance and blows of the sword."

The Norman archers and crossbowmen loosed their shafts, and cut down many of the English defenders in the front line. But Harold's men stood their ground, blocking the arrows as best they could with their leather shields. Then came William's foot soldiers, scrambling up the hill to come within hand-to-hand fighting range of the shield-wall. Harold's housecarles, swinging the terrible two-handed battle-axes, cut easily through the light shields and thin mail of these soldiers, while the rest of the English repelled them with spears and javelins, and with stones slung from forked sticks. Whenever an Englishman fell, the Normans taunted the enemy exultantly; when a Norman perished, the English shouted back. But neither side understood the speech of the other, so many choice insults were wasted on the wind.

Again and again the Normans battered against the wall of shields, but it stood firm, and "they could not penetrate the thick wood of English spears." Harold, cheering his men on, felt that victory was in his grasp. The wall was holding! The Normans were being forced back!

William now ordered his cavalry into action. Up the hill came the horsemen, to be met by a furious hail of lances, darts, throwing-axes, and stone-tipped clubs. The cavalry crashed against the wall of shields and was thrown back.

A fosse, or ditch, crossed the plain. The Normans had passed the fosse, but now the English began to press forward, still keeping their formation, and forced the Norman knights back toward the ditch. Wace tells us, "The English drove the Normans before them until they made them fall back upon this fosse, overthrowing into it horses and men. Many were to be seen falling therein, rolling one over the other, with their faces to the earth, and unable to rise. Many of the English, also, whom the Normans drew down along with them, died there. At no time during the day's battle did so many Normans die as perished in that fosse. So those said who saw the dead."

It was a dark moment for the Normans. They began to mill in panic. Duke William's half-brother, Bishop Odo of Bayeux, tried to rally them. As a man of God, Odo was forbidden by church law to wield spear or sword in battle. But he loved fighting all the same, and carried a short mace, spiked with steel, a deadly weapon but not a forbidden one. Riding on a white horse, and wearing a bishop's white robes under his armor, Odo raised high his mace and shouted, "Stand fast! Stand fast! Be quiet and move not! Fear nothing, for if God please, we shall conquer yet!"

Bishop Odo's words lifted the Norman hearts. But no sooner did they begin to fight with vigor again than new fear struck them. Word passed from man to man: Duke William had been slain! Duke William had fallen!

The Normans were plunged into fresh despair. They turned, began to flee in confusion. Seeing their hated enemies retreating, some of Harold's soldiers gave pursuit, thus breaking the shield-wall. The housecarles stood firm, understanding the king's defensive strategy, but the exuberant and untrained peasants swarmed forward and chased the fleeing Normans down the hill, slaying many of them.

Suddenly the voice of Duke William was heard, booming out in unmistakable tones.

"Look at me, all of you!" the massive Norman cried. "I still live, and with God's help I will conquer! What folly has driven you to flight? If you flee, not one of you will escape death."

The Normans turned. There stood their duke, his helmet off, his head bared so they might all see his face and know he still lived. Norman spirits soared. The horsemen rallied, and wheeled round. The Englishmen who had given pursuit down the hill were cut off and hacked to pieces. Nearly a thousand of Harold's men died in a few moments, it is said.

King Harold himself had remained atop the hill, with his housecarles. His angry shouts had not served to keep the peasants back, and now he had to witness their destruction. A Norse saga relates that then, for the first time, King

The English defend the hill

Harold noticed the bag of holy relics tied to Duke William's banner.

"What is that tied to William's standard?" Harold asked.

A man near him told him that they were the relics on which he had sworn. And Harold said quietly to his brother Gyrth, "It may be that we need not then expect victory in this battle."

Still an unbroken wall of English shields confronted the Normans as they made their way back up the hill to renew the struggle. The battle was far from over. According to Wace:

> From nine o'clock in the morning, when the combat began, till three o'clock came, the battle was up and

down, this way and that, and no one knew who would conquer and win the land. Both sides stood so firm and fought so well that no one could guess which would prevail. The Norman archers with their bows shot thickly upon the English; but they covered themselves with their shields, so that the arrows could not reach their bodies, nor do any mischief, however true was their aim, or however well they shot.

Duke William saw that his heretofore invincible archers were failing to cut the English down. He issued a new order: the archers must "shoot their arrows upward into the air, so that they might fall on their enemies' heads, and strike their faces."

The scheme was a great success. Out of the sky came a hail of sharp arrows, and many an Englishman fell. One of the victims was King Harold himself. Wace tells how "an arrow, that had thus been shot upward, struck Harold above his right eye, and put it out. In his agony he drew the arrow and threw it away, breaking it with his hands, and the pain to his head was so great that he leaned upon his shield."

It may be that this never actually happened. Recently the historian Charles H. Gibbs-Smith has done research into the old story, and he has found that the earliest account of the battle, written by William of Jumièges in 1070, simply says, "Harold himself . . . fell covered with deadly wounds." And the Bayeux Tapestry, woven no later than the 1080's, does not seem to show Harold being struck in the eye with an arrow, but merely being cut down by a Norman sword. The first reference to the arrow-in-the-eye comes from the tale of William of Malmesbury, written in 1125, which said, "When Harold fell, from having his brain pierced with an arrow, the flight of the English ceased not until night."

In any event, Harold was wounded, and the news threw fear into English ranks. But the half-blinded king fought on, desperately trying to hold the shield-wall together. In another part of the field Harold's brother Gyrth came face-to-face with Duke William, and thrust his spear at him, and killed the Norman's horse. William cut Gyrth down with a savage blow and left him dead on the field. Leofwine, Harold's other brother, perished also.

Then the Normans pressed inward, finding weak spots in the English wall. One party of Normans broke through as far as Harold's banner, where Harold himself still fought, "defending himself to the utmost," according to Wace. "But he was sorely wounded in the eye by the arrow, and suffered grievous pain from the blow. An armed man came in the throng of the battle, and struck him on his helmet, and beat him to the ground; and as he sought to recover himself, a knight beat him down again, striking him on the thick of his thigh, down to the bone." The fallen king died, struck dead as he lay wounded. Says William of Malmesbury, "For which shameful and cowardly action, the soldier who did the deed was branded with ignominy by William, and dismissed from the service."

The King of England was dead. In that moment the English cause was lost.

But atop the hill Harold's housecarles grimly fought. An English tradition held that no true warrior survived his lord. They were bound to remain, and fight, if necessary, to the death. They could not flee.

The loss of Harold left the English without a leader,

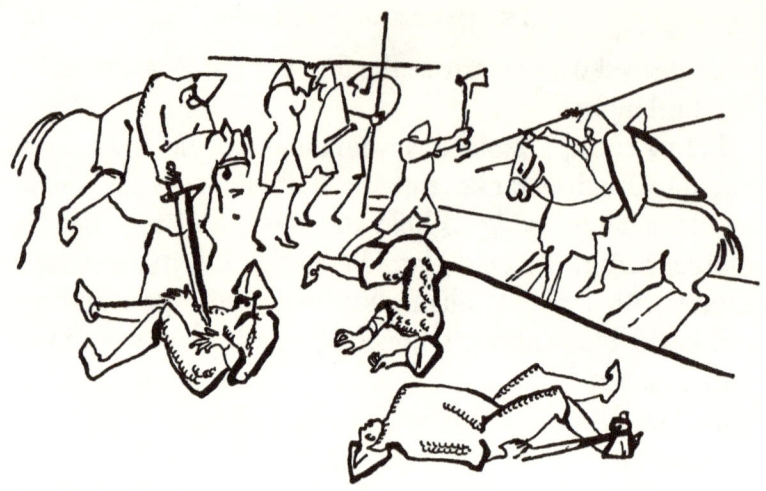

Harold is killed

and it was a grave lack. Duke William quickly took advantage of the situation.

At Stamford Bridge, King Harold had broken Harold Hardrada's shield-wall by pretending a retreat, and luring the Norsemen out of their formation. If Harold had lived at Hastings, it is unlikely that he would have let himself be deceived by the same strategy he had employed so well at the earlier battle. But Harold was dead, and the English fell into William's trap.

Wace writes:

> The Normans arranged to draw off, and pretend to flee, till the English should pursue and scatter themselves over the field. . . . The Normans little by little fled, the English following them. As the one fell back, the other pressed after. And when the Frenchmen retreated, the English thought and cried out that the men of France fled, and would never return.
>
> Thus they were deceived by the pretended flight, and great mischief thereby befell them; for if they had

not moved from their position, it is not likely that they would have been conquered at all; but like fools they broke their lines and pursued.

The Normans were to be seen following up their stratagem, retreating slowly as to draw the English further on. As they still flee, the English pursue; they push out their lances and stretch forth their hatchets; following the Normans, as they go rejoicing in the success of their scheme, and scattering themselves over the plain.

And the English meantime jeered and insulted their foes with words. "Cowards," they cried, "you came hither in an evil hour, wanting our lands, and seeking to seize our property, fools that ye were to come! Normandy is too far off, and you will not easily reach it. It is of little use to run back; unless you can cross the sea at a leap, or can drink it dry, your sons and daughters are lost to you."

Suddenly, as one man, the Normans halted and swung about. The pursuers now became the pursued. Cut off, trapped, the English perished by the hundreds in the melee.

Those Englishmen who had not been fooled still fought with vigor and bravery. Wace writes of one,

> An Englishman who much annoyed the Normans, continually assaulting them with a keen-edged hatchet. He had a helmet made of wood, which he had fastened down to his coat, and laced round his neck, so that no blows could reach his head. The ravage he was making was seen by a gallant Norman knight, who rode a horse that neither fire nor water could stop in its career, when its master urged it on. The knight spurred, and his horse carried him on well till he

charged the Englishman, striking him over the helmet, so that it fell down over his eyes; and as he stretched out his hand to raise it and uncover the face, the Norman cut off his right hand, so that his hatchet fell to the ground. Another Norman sprang forward and eagerly seized the prize with both his hands, but he kept it little space, and paid dearly for it, for as he stooped to pick up the hatchet, an Englishman with his long-handled axe struck him over the back, breaking all his bones, so that his entrails and lungs gushed forth.

In the thick of everything was Duke William. Of him writes William of Malmesbury:

> William too was equally ready to encourage by his voice and by his presence; to be the first to rush forward; to attack the thickest of the foe. Thus everywhere raging, everywhere furious, he lost three choice horses, which were that day pierced under him. The dauntless spirit and vigor of the intrepid general, however, still persisted.

Though often in danger, William was not wounded at all that day. He rallied his men again and again. A second time the Normans staged a feigned retreat, and a second time many English were taken in by it. The army of the dead King Harold was being cut to pieces. Still the housecarles held the top of the hill, and Harold's banner still fluttered high.

As night fell the Normans closed in to finish the job. Swinging their great axes, the housecarles were cut down nearly to the last man. Their courage broke at last. Harold, they knew, was dead. His cause and theirs was lost. The

English survivors began to retreat into the forest that lay behind Senlac hill.

The Normans followed. And now it was their turn to fall victim to an English trap. For behind the English lines lay a concealed ravine, into which hundreds of the Norman horses thundered, tumbling in confusion. In the half-light of dusk the English, who had been fleeing, returned and, with great war whoops, slew the Norman knights who had blundered into the ravine and who now lay helplessly pinned beneath their fallen horses.

It was the last flourish of English strength at Hastings that day. The English forces were dispersed by Norman reinforcements coming up from the rear. The survivors slipped away into the darkness of the forest, or else remained, locked in single combat with Norman knights.

As night finally descended, Duke William returned to the main scene of battle. The dead and the dying lay everywhere, English dead and Norman dead heaped in confusion. Somewhere in the midst of the field, among the hundreds of bodies, lay that of King Harold and those of his brothers Gyrth and Leofwine. Many other noble Englishmen lay there as well. Some ancient aristocratic families had been wholly wiped out that day. Of all the English noblemen who had fought at Hastings, only one is known to have survived, Esegar the chamberlain, who was wounded early in the day and carried from the field.

Some scattered fighting still went on. English peasants, bitter over their king's defeat, lurked in dark places on the field, clubbing isolated Normans down with their crude weapons. But there was no doubt about who the victor had been on the field that day.

William knelt, and, says Wace, "returned thanks to God,

and in his pride ordered his standard to be brought and set up on high where the English standard had stood; and that was the signal of his having conquered and beaten down the foe. And he ordered his tent to be raised on the spot among the dead, and had his meat brought thither, and his supper prepared there."

He took off his armor. The barons and knights, pages and squires, came and took the helmet from his head and the armor from his back. They saw the signs of heavy blows that had landed on the duke's shield, and saw the dents in his helmet. And they praised Duke William for his courage, his strength, and his skill as a warrior. "And the Duke stood meanwhile among them of noble stature and mien, and rendered thanks to the King of Glory, through whom he had the victory; and thanked the knights around him, mourning also frequently for the dead. And he ate and drank among the dead, and made his bed that night upon the field."

As he slept in triumph amid the carnage, William was still merely Duke of Normandy, not yet King of England. The great prize, though, would soon be in his grasp, for both the Harolds were dead, and all the other sons of Godwin. A change was coming for England, a change of masters and a change of ways. Men from beyond the sea would govern now, and, as the Norse poet Thorkil Skallason sang,

> Cold heart and bloody hand
> Now rule the English land.

VII

THE AFTERMATH OF CONQUEST

Dawn BROKE OVER SOUTHERN ENGLAND. It was Sunday morning, the fifteenth of October, 1066. William of Normandy had shattered England's might in ten hours of bloody fighting.

Hushed, stunned by their defeat, the English returned for the bodies of their dead. William of Poitiers, a Norman chaplain who wrote a book called *The Deeds of William, Duke of the Normans and King of the English* in 1071, declared, "It would have been just if wolves and vultures had devoured the flesh of these English who had rightly incurred their doom, and if the fields had received their unburied bones. But such a fate seemed cruel to the duke, and he allowed all who wished to do so to collect the bodies for burial."

One of those who came for her dead was Gytha, sister of King Cnut, wife to Earl Godwin. She had had three of her sons die at Hastings, Harold the King, Gyrth, Leofwine. She offered William Harold's weight in gold for the body of the dead king. The story goes that William refused to let her have Harold's body, for, he said, a man who had broken a sacred oath did not deserve Christian burial.

Then came two monks from Waltham Abbey, which King Harold had founded not long before his death. They, too, asked for the fallen king's corpse, and they, too, were refused by William. Meanwhile Edith, called Edith of the Swan Neck, who had been the beloved of Harold, went onto the field and searched for him, and finally found his stripped, bleeding body. According to one story, she and the monks from Waltham succeeded in carrying the king's body off to be buried. Another tale has it that William discovered them and prevented it, and ordered a half-Norman English knight named William Malet, a friend of Harold's, to bury him under a cairn of rocks at Hastings. Only later, so it is said, did William relent and allow Harold to be be buried at Waltham.

William, too, had dead to bury, and that Sunday and the day that followed it were spent in the sad task. But other work beckoned to him.

Harold of England was dead, and Harold of Norway also. William of Normandy could claim the English throne by right of conquest, if not by right of descent. One battle, though, does not conquer an entire land. All England still stretched before the Normans, a land leaderless but not yet crushed. There were powerful men still to contend with. The northern earls, Edwin and Morcar, had not been at Hastings, and still lived to pose possible menace to the Normans. There was the whole city of London, rich and strong. The task of subduing England remained, William knew.

For five days he waited at Hastings, resting his men and sending for reinforcements from Normandy to replace the men killed in battle. He hoped also that the English gathered in London would send a messenger, inviting him peacefully to come and be their king.

No messenger came. Word had come to London of King Harold's defeat, and the leaders of the realm were gathering there to discuss the situation. Earls Edwin and Morcar, who had been marching southward at a slow pace to come to Harold's aid, went now to London, after placing Harold's widow, their sister Aldgyth, in safety at Chester. Both of England's archbishops, Stigand of Canterbury and Eldred of York, were at London also, along with such surviving nobles as Esegar the chamberlain.

A meeting of the witan was held—though many of its members who had elected Harold king in January now lay dead on the field at Hastings. It was decided to offer the crown to the only remaining member of the old Saxon royal family, Edgar the Atheling, who was still a child. Edgar was elected, but no formal coronation was held. Shrewd Archbishop Stigand suggested a wait-and-see policy.

When William learned that the witan had chosen the boy Edgar and not himself, he decided to leave Hastings. He placed one of his best lieutenants in charge of the castle at Hastings. William went first to Romney, where some of his men had been killed by townspeople on the day of the Norman landing. There, William of Poitiers writes, "he punished at his pleasure those who had previously killed some of his men."

William's next stop was Dover. This important coastal town had been fortified by Harold, and a large garrison had been left there to defend it. But the English panicked at the approach of William. We can read the story in the account of William of Poitiers:

> Then he marched to Dover, which had been reported impregnable and held by a large force. The English, stricken with fear at his approach, had confidence neither in their ramparts nor in the natural strength of the site, nor in the number of their troops. This castle is situated on a rock adjoining the sea, and it is raised up by nature and so strongly fortified that it stands like a straight wall as high as an arrow's flight. Its side is washed by the sea.

Despite these advantages, the English garrison agreed to surrender unconditionally. William of Poitiers continues:

> Our men, greedy for booty, set fire to the castle, and the greater part of it was soon enveloped in flames. The duke, unwilling that those who had offered to surrender should suffer loss, gave them a recompense in money for the damage of the castle and their property; and he would have severely punished those who had started the fire if their numbers and base conditions had not prevented their detection.

Having taken possession of the castle at Dover, William spent eight days rebuilding and enlarging its fortifications after the Norman manner. Meanwhile, "owing to the foul water and bad food," many of William's knights were stricken by dysentery. Some died and many were weakened almost to the point of death.

William left them behind. With his healthy troops, he marched onward to the important cathedral city of Canterbury. The townsfolk of Canterbury were not minded to taste William's might, and they hurried out to surrender to him, meeting him on the road while he was still some distance away. William entered Canterbury in triumph.

There he, too, fell ill—perhaps with dysentery, perhaps with gout. He had been under great stress all year, and the events of the last few weeks had tested even his fierce strength. His conquest of England came to a temporary halt, then, while he rested in Canterbury for some weeks.

The notables of England were reacting in different ways to William's successes. A few backed the right of Edgar the Atheling to be crowned, but they did not speak up very loudly. Some, like Edwin and Morcar, outwardly supported Edgar, but actually had no real intention of backing him. What they really wanted, it appeared, was a deal with William, giving him the southern half of the kingdom and keeping Northumbria and Mercia for themselves. Another important figure was Queen Edith, the widow of Edward the Confessor and sister to the dead King Harold. Queen Edith evidently found it safer to throw in her lot with William than to trust to the mercies of Edwin and Morcar. While William rested at Canterbury, Edith sent word to him that she would recognize him as king, and would surrender to him her city of Winchester.

It was encouraging news for the Norman duke. As soon as he was healthy enough to mount a horse, he resumed his slow journey northward.

William sent five hundred men to test the defenses of London. They approached the city from the south, entering the district known as Southwark. London proper lay on the far side of the River Thames, and a wooden bridge was the only way to get there. William's men attempted to cross the bridge, but suffering heavy losses, they were beaten back by the soldiers of London.

The Norman duke realized that it would be costly and hazardous to try to force an entry into London. He decided instead to lay waste to the countryside surrounding the city, and to force London to submit.

The Normans began their scorched-earth campaign by burning Southwark. One of the buildings destroyed was a great mansion that had belonged first to Earl Godwin and then to King Harold. Retreating, the invaders ravaged a broad strip of territory south of the Thames, forging westward through the shires of Surrey, northern Hampshire, and Berkshire. As he moved, the Norman made it perfectly clear what his attitude toward the English would be: he would be just and merciful to those who surrendered peacefully, but he would be ruthless to those who opposed him.

The lesson sank in. Still William plundered and destroyed, methodically sacking town after town. When he reached Wallingford, a town about fifty miles west of London, William and his men crossed the Thames and camped on the north bank, in Oxfordshire.

It was his plan to circle back eastward now, laying waste to the country north of the Thames just as he had done to that to the south, thus encircling London with a ring of devastation. But it was not necessary for him to complete the circle. He had moved less than halfway back in his course of destruction, and had come to the town of Berkhamsted, when a party of English noblemen and clergy rode out of London to speak with him and invite him to be their king.

William had had a good idea that the invitation would be forthcoming. He knew that a hot debate was raging in London. Archbishop Stigand, the Earls Edwin and Morcar, and a horde of other influential Englishmen had been discussing the national situation all during the month of

November. Among them were certain Normans and Frenchmen like Robert FitzWymarc, who had lived in London since the days of Edward the Confessor, and these men argued in favor of recognizing William as the new king.

The chief supporter of the Norman was Archbishop Stigand. This may seem strange. After all, William had told the pope that one of his chief motives for making war against Harold was to remove the excommunicated Stigand from his cathedral seat at Canterbury. Why should Stigand back the claim of the very man who had vowed to expel him?

Stigand was a good politician. The clever archbishop sensed that if he made his peace with William, and fought to have the Norman duke placed on England's throne, Duke William might very well spare him.

And so it happened that while William was still at Wallingford, Archbishop Stigand quietly rode out to visit him. The archbishop knelt before the duke, placed his hands in those of William, and swore to be faithful. Stigand vowed that he would return to London and persuade the others to give William the crown.

Stigand kept his vow. At Berkhamsted, twenty-five miles west of London, a party of Englishmen came to Duke William. Archbishop Stigand was among them, and the Earls Edwin and Morcar, and the boy Edgar the Atheling, England's uncrowned "king," and Archbishop Eldred of York, and many others. One by one they made formal submission to William. William of Poitiers writes, "And it was very unwise that they had not done so before. . . . And they delivered hostages, and swore oaths to him; and he vowed to them that he would be a loving lord to them."

Despite William's vow to be "a loving lord," he did not

prevent his men from plundering the rest of the way to London. When the Normans reached London, some Londoners were unwilling to accept William as their lord. There was fighting at the city gates. But Stigand, Edwin, Morcar, and Edgar the Atheling made peace. London surrendered, and William entered the greatest city of England.

William lost no time insuring that London would stay under Norman control. One of his first acts was to have a Norman-style fortress built within the city. It was the beginning of the great pile of masonry known today as the Tower of London.

On Christmas Day, 1066, Duke William of Normandy went to Westminster Abbey for the ceremony of crowning. Edward the Confessor lay buried there; Harold of Wessex had been crowned there less than twelve months before.

The coronation rites were once again performed by Archbishop Eldred of York. Archbishop Stigand, who had played so important a role in bringing William to the throne so fast, had perhaps expected to perform the rites himself, as was his privilege. But William, like Harold before him, did not care to risk the displeasure of God by letting an excommunicated archbishop crown him. Stigand stood by in disappointment, and played only a minor role in the colorful ceremony.

Within the impressive new abbey, Duke William ascended the throne of Edward the Confessor. The holy rites were uttered, and the Norman's head anointed with oil. Instead of donning the old crown of the English kings, which had been worn by Cnut, Ethelred the Unready, Edward the Confessor, and Harold, William was given a new crown, glittering with precious stones.

There was one unusual part of the ceremony. William

had come to the throne not by inheritance but by conquest. He found it necessary to make it seem as though he had been "elected" king by the people.

So those assembled in the abbey were asked if they accepted William as their king. Archbishop Eldred put the question in English, and Bishop Geoffrey of Coutances asked it in Norman French.

"Yes! Yes!" came the ringing replies.

Norman knights had been stationed outside the abbey as guards. When they heard the loud shouting, they thought a riot had broken out within and that William might be in danger. They reacted with an old Norman technique for quelling a riot. They set fire to the wooden buildings surrounding the abbey.

As smoke curled through the building, many of those who had come to witness the coronation rushed out into the open to save themselves from the flames. With drawn swords, the Norman guards forced their way into the abbey to come to their duke's aid.

Greatly to their surprise, they found the coronation proceeding as scheduled. And so it was that with panic swirling about him, in fire and smoke, in confusion and terror, the grandchild of the tanner of Falaise added to his title of Duke of Normandy that of King of England.

MOST LIKELY few Englishmen realized the importance of what had been done that day at Westminster.

Exactly fifty years before, another foreigner—Cnut—had become King of England. But England had not changed. It was Cnut who changed, rather, becoming an Englishman by customs if not by birth. Cnut, though a Dane, had maintained all the old laws of England. He had ruled like a native king, and his ministers had mostly been Englishmen. After Cnut and the short reigns of his two sons Harold Harefoot and Harthacnut, the throne passed into the hands of Englishmen again. Nothing had changed, and it was as if Danes had never ruled in England.

It was otherwise with King William and his Normans.

All England would change. The laws, the customs, even the language, would change and never be the same again.

Nobody in England fully realized this on Christmas Day of 1066, perhaps not even King William himself. He was far from being king of all England that day. Only the southeastern part of the country had actually accepted his rule. Although Edwin and Morcar had promised their loyalty, that was no guarantee that the tough-minded men of northern England would agree to bow to a Norman. Even in London itself, William was not popular among the Englishmen.

The throne was his. Now he had to make England accept the fact that he was king.

He was faced with an immediate dilemma. King William did not want to confiscate the lands of his new subjects. But he had promised to pay the men of his conquering army by giving them English land. How could he give land to Normans without necessarily taking it from English?

He could begin at least by taking away the land of those Englishmen who had fought against him at Hastings. He did this and made it seem just by employing an ingenious legal argument. He declared that since he was the rightful heir of Edward the Confessor, Harold had never really been king but only a usurper. The nine months of Harold's reign had simply been an interlude of confusion and misrule.

The Battle of Hastings had not been a clash between two nations, but the suppression of a rebellion against England's lawful king, William.

Therefore Harold's men were nothing but rebels. They deserved to lose their land. King William issued a decree taking away the holdings of all those Englishmen "who stood against me in battle, and were slain there."

He distributed the lands of these dead knights among his own Norman followers. Each man got something, according to his rank and the number of soldiers he had brought with him to the battle. For example, one Guillaume de Garonne was made lord of eighteen villages, and one Guillaume de Percy was given eighty villages. The town of Alnwick was awarded to Ives de Vesey, along with the granddaughter of the Englishman who had ruled there earlier, to be the Norman's wife. And so it went, Normans great and small taking possession of English lands and moving into English manors. Many of the Normans sent to the home country for their friends and relatives, who moved lock, stock, and barrel to dwell in this rich land. As French-speaking strangers began to swarm into England, the English watched with alarm. Land-hungry Normans scurried everywhere, while the English sang such mocking jingles as this:

> *William of Coningsby*
> *Came out of Brittany,*
> *With his wife Tiffany*
> *And his maid Manfas,*
> *And his dog Hardigras.*

King William tried to be lenient toward the conquered English, however. The widows and children of Harold's fallen knights were granted pensions by the new king, and in some cases were allowed to keep a portion of the lands that once had been theirs. Harold's surviving supporters were allowed to "buy back their lands" by paying a heavy fine to King William and doing him homage. None the less, in the south of England, four-fifths of the land passed from English hands to the hands of Normans.

Many of those who had been important in the reigns of Edward and Harold were allowed to keep their power. Some of these were men of Norman descent who had lived in England for twenty years or more, men like Robert Fitz-Wymarc and Ralf the Staller. Archbishop Stigand was allowed to remain on at Canterbury, despite William's promise to the pope. Edwin and Morcar were permitted to keep their earldoms, as was Waltheof, son of Earl Siward of Northumbria, to whom King Edward had given extensive lands in east-central England.

William also invented some new earldoms and put them in the hands of his own men. His childhood friend William Fitz-Osbern was named Earl of Hereford. The king's half-brother, Bishop Odo of Bayeux, became the first Earl of Kent. Such Norman leaders as Hugh of Montfort and William of Warenne were given lesser titles.

For a short while after his coronation King William remained at Barking, just outside the city. Many English thegns came to him there and paid homage, including Earls Edwin and Morcar. Another who came was Copsi, who in May had taken part in Tostig's ill-fated invasion of England. William rewarded Copsi by making him an earl and giving him substantial lands in the north of England.

From Barking, William set out to inspect the conquered part of England. He traveled in state through his new domain, accepting the grudging homage of the English and pointing out the places where he wanted castles to be built as garrison posts for his troops.

By March, 1067, only six months after Harold's downfall, King William deemed it safe to return for a visit to Normandy. He had left his wife there and was eager to see her. Besides, it was unsafe for him, as duke, to remain away from Normandy too long lest he lose his homeland to another while busy subduing a foreign country.

William set sail from Pevensey, the same port where he had first set foot on English soil at the end of September. He was accompanied by many English notables, among them Edwin and Morcar, Archbishop Stigand, Edgar the Atheling, and young Earl Waltheof. William took these figures along to show how complete his triumph had been over England—so total that he could carry English earls as "baggage" in his train.

With him also sailed those Norman and French knights who did not care to make their permanent homes in England. William had paid these men handsomely, weighing them down with gold and silver that the English had been forced to contribute as tax, and the knights had also acquired much through their own private looting. So it was a majestic and glittering party that crossed the Channel to Normandy that spring. The ships had hoisted white sails, the traditional symbol of victory, and aboard them rode Norman knights who six months ago had left home with no possessions other than their swords and horses and now returned as wealthy men.

William was wildly welcomed at his capital of Rouen. Despite the late-winter chill, cheering throngs lined the streets to shout their acclaim. He came bearing gifts for the churches of Normandy: gold and silver ornaments, priestly robes embroidered in cloth-of-gold and worked with precious gems. He sent other such gifts to all the churches in Europe that had prayed for his victory, and to the pope went Harold's gold-encrusted, bejeweled banner of the Fighting Man.

For eight months William remained in Normandy. In his absence England was governed jointly by William Fitz-Osbern and Odo of Bayeux. During that time the first rebellion against King William broke out in England.

It was led not by an Englishman but by one of William's own barons, Count Eustace of Boulogne. Eustace had fought at Hastings, but he felt he had not been sufficiently rewarded. He was jealous of the influence and power granted to Odo of Bayeux. Eustace felt that he and not Odo should have been given the important Kentish town of Dover.

Eustace joined forces with the men of Dover. They had given up hope of ever seeing an Englishman as their ruler again, but at the very least they seemed to prefer Eustace to Odo. So while Odo was absent from Dover, Eustace and his Kentish allies broke into revolt. But the Norman garrison at Dover easily quelled the disturbance. The English rebels were scattered, and Count Eustace sailed back to his own country in defeat.

William did not bother to return to England when news of this shortlived uprising reached him. He was still enjoying the celebrations in Normandy. He traveled from town to Norman town, accompanied by his wife Matilda. Everywhere the people hailed him, for he had brought great wealth to Normandy. All of England now lay open for Normans to seek their fortune in.

The Normans were awed, too, by the splendor of the

treasures William had brought from England—the costly church garments, the gold and silver treasures, the elegant illuminated manuscripts so lovingly set down by English monks. Perhaps, too, William had brought with him the great gold ingot of Harold Hardrada, although there is no record of this. And the Normans stared in wonder at the golden-haired young Englishmen, Edwin and Morcar and Waltheof and Edgar, so different in appearance from the dark-haired folk of Normandy.

Summer and fall, King-Duke William enjoyed his triumph. But as cold winds began to snap through the vineyards and fields of Normandy there came disturbing news. The English were restless. Odo and William Fitz-Osbern had ruled harshly and had won no love in the conquered land. There was danger of a revolt in the part of England that acknowledged William's sovereignty, and the still unconquered districts to the north and west were making menacing gestures of defiance.

William left Matilda in charge of governing Normandy. For the first time, he named his eldest son Robert to assist her, though he was barely into his teens. On the night of December 6, 1067—a bitter-cold night—William set sail once again for England.

MATTERS WERE TENSE in England. By their thoughtless cruelty William Fitz-Osbern and Odo had wrecked the policy of leniency by which King William had hoped to win the cooperation of his English subjects. The peaceful blending of Englishman and Norman into a new Anglo-Norman race was endangered.

King William went first to London. He was received well enough there—perhaps the Londoners were glad to see him after having had a taste of the rule of his two lieutenants—and he celebrated the first anniversary of his crowning with a peaceful Christmas feast.

Then he turned to deal with those who would oppose his rule.

One center of opposition was western Wessex, the onetime property of Godwin and Harold. The western towns of Wessex had formed a league and had sworn to resist William.

The leader of this league was the town of Exeter, where Gytha, mother of King Harold and sister of King Cnut, dwelled. Gytha herself was inspiring the revolt.

King William met the challenge directly. He sent a message to Exeter, asking the important men of the town to come to him and take an oath of loyalty. They refused, replying that they would neither swear an oath to the king nor receive him within the walls of Exeter. They would, however, be willing to visit London and pay tribute to William.

"It is not my custom," William answered, "to receive my subjects on such conditions."

He led an army in person to Exeter. It is interesting that there were English soldiers in this army, the first time on record that English and Norman soldiers joined ranks in the same force. Long before King William reached Exeter, the thegns of that city had lost their courage and abandoned their defiance. Hurriedly they scurried from behind Exeter's walls and met William on the road four miles from the town. They begged for peace, offered hostages, and agreed to open the city gates and allow William to enter without opposition.

The ordinary folk of Exeter had more valor than their leaders. They refused to abide by the terms of surrender and prepared to defend their town against the king.

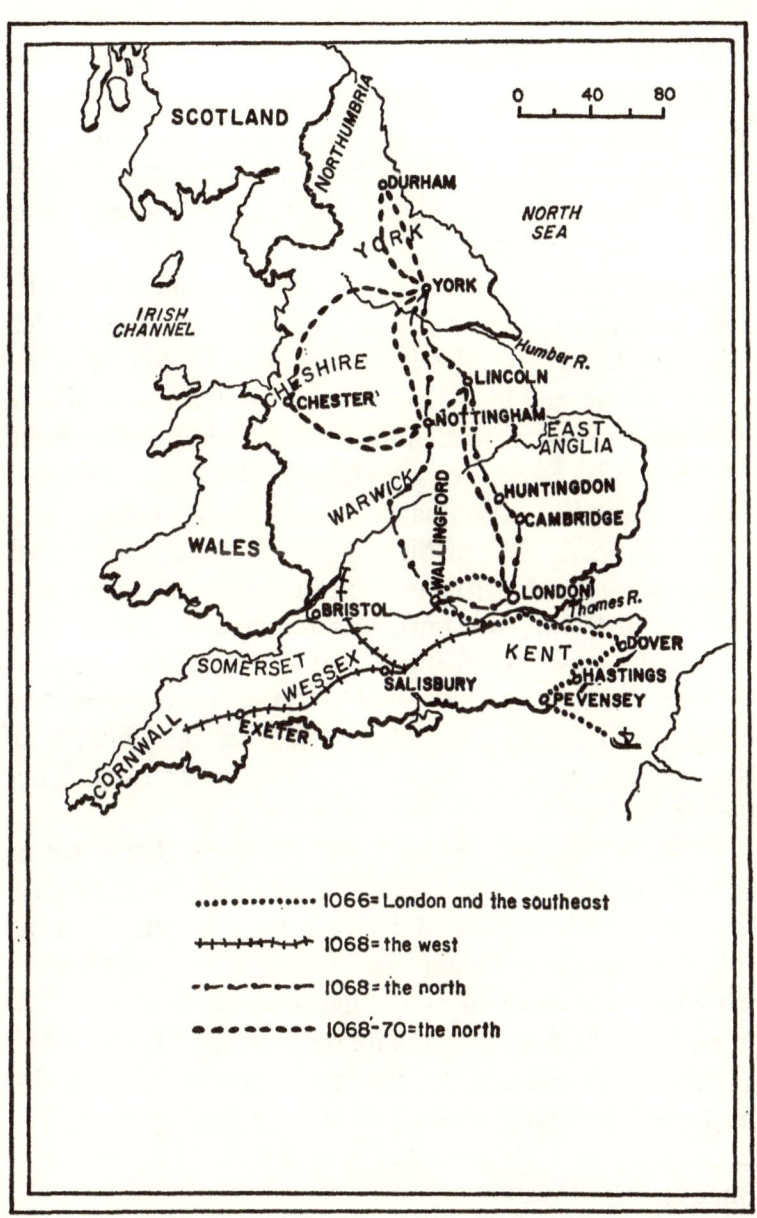

William's successive conquests in England

William was furious. He rode up to the gates of Exeter at the head of five hundred men. Armed Englishmen looked down at him from the walls. Angrily William sent for one of the hostages given him by the thegns of Exeter and ordered him to be blinded in front of the city as an example to the others.

King William had hoped to frighten the men of Exeter into surrendering without a struggle. Instead, their determination hardened. The king laid siege to the town for eighteen days, and for all his military prowess was unable to gain entry. Finally, with hunger threatening the besieged city, surrender came. The people of Exeter issued forth and threw themselves at William's feet to beg his pardon.

In those early days of his reign King William was quick to show mercy. He forgave Exeter, not even raising the amount of tribute the town was required to pay. A Norman castle was erected there, and William left a garrison to keep the town under control. Gytha, Harold's mother, escaped by fishing boat, taking with her the children of King Harold by his mistress Edith of the Swan Neck. They fled to Ireland.

William marched westward, into Cornwall. There was no serious opposition here, and in short order western England was made to sumbit to William. He put Cornwall into the hands of his other half-brother, Robert of Mortain, who kept Cornwall in check. Meanwhile, a few months later, Harold's three illegitimate sons returned from Ireland at the head of an army of Danes and Irishmen. They landed at Bristol and were driven off by the townspeople. The same happened at Somerset, and the invaders withdrew once again to Ireland.

Southern England was now under William's sway,

Gytha flees with Harold's children to Ireland

from Kent to Cornwall. In the spring of 1068 William staged a ceremony that symbolized his growing power in England. He brought Duchess Matilda out of Normandy and had her crowned as Queen of England.

England had never had a crowned queen before. The Anglo-Saxon word *cwene* simply meant "woman." The wife of the king had borne the title of "Lady" and had worn no crown. Matilda arrived accompanied by a host of Norman nobles and bishops, and on Whit Sunday, 1068, was crowned in Westminster Abbey by Archbishop Eldred of York. In less than a year, she gave birth to a son on English soil. His name was Henry, and he would someday be King of England after his father and brother.

In the summer of 1068 King William had new troubles in his realm.

Edwin and Morcar, those oddly flexible northern earls whose chief loyalty was not to England but to themselves, were in a mood of resentment. At the time of William's coronation the new king had promised to allow them to keep such possessions as they had held before the Conquest. But King William had given some of Morcar's land to Copsi. He had placed other men, Normans, in positions of high power in Edwin's territory. And though he had promised to give one of his daughters to Edwin as wife, William had backed down on the pledge.

Disgruntled, Edwin and Morcar left William's court and went to York to stir up rebellion against the king. At the same time Edgar the Aetheling, who was required to remain where William could keep an eye on him, fled also and, with his mother and sisters, took refuge with King Malcolm in Scotland. Suddenly the whole north of England, which had never really accepted William as king, was on the verge of explosion.

William moved with typical force. He marched northward for the first time. At Warwick he planted a strongly defended castle, and built another at Nottingham. Edwin and Morcar, realizing they stood no chance against the king, quickly surrendered, and William entered York without a battle. He built a castle there, too. Next, he sent the Bishop of Durham into Scotland to negotiate with King Malcolm. Malcolm had been thinking of invading England, but the bishop convinced him it would be folly, and the Scottish king swore fealty to William.

On his return southward King William built three more castles, at Lincoln, Huntingdon, and Cambridge. For the moment, the north was quiet again. Not for long.

Trouble started when the powerful men of the north began to fight with one another. Copsi, William's man, was regarded as an upstart by the old families of Northumbria. After five weeks of rule, Copsi was slain by Oswulf, a descendant of the ancient ruling house of Bernicia. Oswulf in turn was murdered in the fall of 1068, and William sold the earldom to an Englishman named Cospatric.

No sooner did Cospatric gain power then he threw in his lot with Edgar the Atheling and backed the exiled prince against William. Angrily William vowed to punish the northerners. He named one of his Flemish followers, Robert of Comines, as Earl of Bernicia and sent him north with a considerable army.

When he reached the town of Durham, Robert of Comines was overtaken by an even larger English army. On January 28, 1069, the English surrounded the town, cut the Norman troops down, and set fire to the house where the new earl was staying. He perished in the flames. Northumbria was in open revolt. The killing of Earl Robert was followed by an English attack on York. The English besieged the Norman castle there and demaded that the people of York acknowledge Edgar the Atheling as their king.

The castle at York was in command of William Malet, the knight who had buried King Harold's body. Malet fought valiantly, and the garrison staved off the rebel attack and managed to send a messenger to King William asking for help.

William duplicated Harold's lightning-fast march to York of several years earlier. He reached the besieged city with incredible swiftness and put the rebels to the sword. After eight days, York was tranquil again. William built a second castle there, putting it in the charge of William

Fitz-Osbern, Earl of Hereford. This ruthless baron launched a bloody attack against the outlying country, quelling the last vestiges of rebellion.

Later in the summer of 1069 there was fresh woe. The sons of King Harold made a second attempt at invasion. They landed near Exeter with sixty-six ships and headed inland. A day-long battle routed them and there were scarcely any survivors. The sons of Harold fled. Some say they went to Denmark, where they were welcomed by King Sweyn Estrithson, their kinsman, who received them in "kind and friendly manner." With them to Denmark fled Harold's daughter—so says the twelfth-century historian Saxo Grammaticus—and King Sweyn "bestowed the young damsel in marriage upon Yaroslav, King of Russia."

"UNEASY LIES THE HEAD that wears a crown," Shakespeare wrote. The crowned head of William of Normandy knew no ease in those years. Revolt and invasion, invasion and revolt—the conquest of England dragged on and on.

No sooner were the sons of Harold defeated than a new enemy presented itself: Sweyn Estrithson himself, the Danish king, coming at last to press his claim to England's throne. Not since the days of his uncle Cnut and his grandfather Sweyn had Danes menaced England, but now, taking advantage of the island's divided state, Sweyn invaded.

He did not come in person, but sent three sons and his brother Osbern, heading a fleet of 240 ships. The Danes came with the encouragement and backing of Edgar the Atheling, Edwin, Morcar, and Waltheof, all of whom preferred even a Danish overlord to the hated William.

The Danes first attacked Dover, but were driven off. They made their way up the east coast of England, along the shores of Kent and East Anglia, without succeeding in making a landing. But as they continued north, they approached the part of England still known as the Danelaw, inhabited for the last two centuries by people of Danish descent. Here the invaders got a friendlier welcome.

The Danes made a landing at the mouth of the River Humber, and were met by a large English army under Waltheof, Edgar the Atheling, and Cospatric. This combined army attacked York, and this time the Norman garrisons could not hold the city. In a strategic error the Normans left their castles to attack the invaders. They were vastly outnumbered and perished nearly to the last man.

It was the worst defeat the Normans had ever suffered in England, or would ever suffer. York was in English-Danish hands, and could have served as a bastion from which the rebels could wrest all northern England from William.

Mysteriously they failed to build on their success. Word reached them that King William was marching northward against them, and they panicked. The Danes withdrew from York without waiting for William's arrival, and legged it back to their ships at anchor in the Humber. They boarded the ships and remained on board, idle and motionless, neither retreating to Denmark nor taking up arms against William.

Faced with the loss of their powerful Danish allies, the English rebels had to hurry into hiding. William, who had been busy suppressing minor revolts in Wessex and Mercia, gathered his forces to move northward and crush the Northumbrian rebels for good and all.

By the time William could move northward, the Danes had wakened from their fit of fear and were once again occupying York. Christmas was drawing near, and the

Danish invaders wished to make merry among their kinsmen of York. William hoped to cut them off, but he was delayed for three weeks by a broken bridge at the River Aire. Finally, a Norman knight named Lisois found a place where it was safe to ford the Aire, and King William's troops crossed over.

The march on York was slow. Cruel winter weather slashed at the Normans. There were unfamiliar forests and marshes to cross. Bands of raiding English rebels harassed them every step of the way.

When William approached York, he learned that the Danes had once again slipped back to their ships. The king now divided his forces into three groups. One corps he sent in to occupy York itself, to rebuild the two fortresses and defend them against any attackers. The second corps was sent off to keep watch over the Danes anchored in the Humber.

William himself commanded the third corps. He intended to track down the English rebels and shatter them, and then to put a permanent end to Northumbria's resistance by laying waste to the entire countryside.

He carried this grim work out for week after week, burning village after villiage, killing or driving away inhabitants and cattle, cutting a swath of destruction from the North Sea to the Irish Channel. It was for this somber exploit, not for his victory at Hastings, that William received the title of Conqueror by which we know him.

Even the Norman chroniclers, who regarded William generally as a just and noble man, were shocked by the Conqueror's vengeance on Northumbria. One wrote:

> Never had William shown so great a cruelty. He gave way shamefully to this vice, and did not trouble

William and his forces plunder Northumbria

to restrain his resentment, striking down innocent and guilty alike with an equal fury. In the anger which carried him away, he caused to be assembled crops, herds and flocks, food and utensils of every kind, and burned them all. In this manner all the sources of life north of the Humber were destroyed. There followed in England a famine so serious and so widespread, the disasters of the famine were so frightful, among a population helpless or disarmed, that more than 100,000 individuals of all ages and of both sexes perished.

More than 100,000 perished! Since the whole population of England at that time was less than 2,000,000, it means that better than one Englishman out of twenty died of famine as a result of William's sack of the north. So terrible was the devastation that nearly two decades later vast stretches of Northumbria were still unpopulated and destroyed.

England was still by no means subdued, even after this havoc. The Danes remained in their ships in the Humber. Since they showed no sign of emerging to do battle, William left them alone and concentrated on the remaining English rebels. He received the submission of Waltheof and Cospatric at Christmastime. In January, 1070, he began a terrible march across the snow-covered uplands of England, from York to Chester in the west, where bands of English and Welsh rebels were harrowing the countryside.

William's army nearly mutinied during the dreadful winter march. The Conqueror compelled them to follow him, winning their loyalty by sharing all their hardships. They reached Chester, crushed the rebels, and built new fortresses. His chief aide in the action at Chester was Hugues of Avranches, nicknamed Hugues-de-Loup, "Hugh the Wolf," for his ferocity. William made Hugues Earl of Chester and left him to complete the task of subjugating Cheshire and Wales. By Easter of 1070, William was at Salisbury, and he released many of his soldiers from service because for the moment there was no serious rebellion anywhere in England.

William moved on to Winchester for his Easter feast. He had three visitors at Winchester: three cardinals of the Catholic Church, sent from Rome by the pope.

William made use of the cardinals in a new coronation ceremony at Winchester. The papal legates once again crowned William King of the English. But they had not come particularly for that purpose. They had come to discuss the embarrassing and ticklish matter of Archbishop Stigand.

It was three and a half years since Harold's death, and yet Stigand still served as Archbishop of Canterbury and Bishop of Winchester, though the pope had never lifted the order of excommunication against him. The time of reckoning had come. King William was in an awkward position, since he could not back Stigand against the pope, and yet was obligated to the archbishop as an ally.

William found a solution. Stigand would have to step down both as Archbishop of Canterbury and as Bishop of Winchester. But he would be allowed to keep all the wealth he had amassed while holding those posts, and William would give him certain lands that would bring him an additional income of 800 pounds sterling a year, a fortune in those days. Stigand grumbled, but had to submit. He died two years later, one of the wealthiest men in England.

William brought out of Normandy his old adviser, Lanfranc, and made that shrewd and learned man Archbishop of Canterbury. At the same time, the king named as Archbishop of York Thomas of Bayeux. The two highest church posts in England now were in the hands of William's men. It was the beginning of the gradual movement that took the English church completely out of the control of the Anglo-Saxon priesthood.

In the spring of 1070 the Danes who had been at anchor in the Humber bestirred themselves. King Sweyn himself came to join them, leading a second fleet. A party of Danes had spent the winter digging in at a new site on the Isle of Ely, building a strong fortified encampment, and it became the headquarters for rebels from all over England, such as the man called Hereward the Wake. Hereward, a thegn of Lincolnshire, had seen action against William the year before, and now became one of the boldest spirits in the rebel camp at the Isle of Ely.

Using Ely as a base, the Danish-English forces struck in sudden raids. The most famous of these was the sack of Peterborough, June 2, 1070. Under the leadership of Hereward the rebels descended on this town, meaning to pillage the monastery because William had given it to a Norman abbot named Turold. In the Anglo-Saxon Chronicle there is this account:

> Then early in the morning all the outlaws came with many ships, and they endeavored to enter the monastery, but the monks withstood them, so that they were not able to get in. Then they set fire to it, and burned all the monks' houses, and all those in the town, save one . . . and the monks came before them and desired peace.
>
> However they gave no heed to them, but went into the monastery, and climbed up to the holy crucifix, took the crown from our Lord's head, which was all of the purest gold, and the footstool of red gold from under his feet. And they climbed up to the steeple, and brought down the table which was hidden there; it was all of gold and silver. They also seized two gilt shrines, and nine of silver, and they carried off fifteen great crosses of gold and silver. And they took so much gold and silver, and so much treasure in money, robes, and books, that no man can compute the amount . . . and afterwards they betook themselves to their ships and went to Ely, where they secured their treasures.

Despite the success of this raid, the Danes did no further harm. King Sweyn Estrithson's heart had never really been bent on conquest. He and William reached an agreement in the summer of 1070, by which the Danes would peacefully depart from England, abandoning the fort at Ely. The Chronicle notes:

> The Danes departed from Ely, carrying with them all the aforesaid treasure. When they were come into

the midst of the sea, there arose a great storm, which dispersed all the ships in which the treasures were; some were driven to Norway, some to Ireland, and others to Denmark.

Though the Danes were gone, Hereward the Wake and the other English rebels refused to quit the base at Ely. They held out for more than a year. Early in 1071, Earl Morcar, who had not yet actually taken up arms against William, joined the rebel force at Ely.

King William laid siege to the rebel stronghold in the summer of 1071. The only route to the island was by a secret path through the fens, or marshes, surrounding it. According to one story, monks on the island betrayed this secret path to William in return for a pledge of their own safety. William took the rebels by surprise, killed many, and captured most of the others.

One of the prisoners taken was Earl Morcar, who was placed under close guard. To liberate him his brother Edwin tried to assemble an army of Englishmen, Welshmen, and Scots, but he met a tragic end. Three brothers, followers of Edwin, treacherously slew him and brought his head to King William, hoping for a generous reward. It is said that William wept at the death of the young English earl and angrily ordered his murderers to be banished.

One of the few who escaped from Ely in 1071 was Hereward the Wake. With a handful of companions he cut his way out, and for some months thereafter waged guerrilla warfare against the Normans. He became a symbol of English courage and resistance, and in the twelfth century legends of his exploits were told by Englishmen the way men of another time talked of such heroes as Davy Crockett and Daniel Boone. Toward the end of his life, though, Hereward came to accept the reality of William's power and submitted to him, even serving in his army.

By the end of 1071 rebellion was ended. Edwin was dead, Morcar a prisoner. The Danes had departed. Waltheof had submitted to William. Edgar the Atheling, last of the old Anglo-Saxon royal line, was a pitiful fugitive in Scotland, where King Molcolm had married the Atheling's sister Margaret.

Every shire of England acknowledged King William as its ruler.

William the Conqueror reigned supreme.

VIII

NORMAN ENGLAND

Now came the time of great change in England. What amounted to a social revolution took place. The old ways yielded, and new patterns appeared in English society.

Some of the changes came faster than King William probably desired. He had hoped to make a gradual transition from the old ways to the new. But the continuing revolts of the English killed that dream. Such men as Edwin, Morcar, and Edgar the Atheling might have smoothed the way for William, but they chose to set their hands against his. As a result, they were driven out, and Norman barons came to rule in their place. The ties with the old England were shattered.

The roots of the Anglo-Saxon governing system survived. The local officials, the county sheriffs, the courts—all these the Conqueror carried over from the old regime. He had to. There were not enough Normans available or willing to take over the responsibilities of government. The Anglo-Saxon system, built up over five or six centuries, kept running on its own momentum and William did not meddle with its finely balanced machinery.

Thus the "hundred courts" survived. A "hundred" was a territorial division of varying size, playing the same part in an English shire or county that a county does in an American state today. Each hundred had its own court, a kind of popular assembly that met in the open air every four weeks to do justice on a local scale.

There were other courts, too—borough courts, shire courts, and private courts under the jurisdiction of great landowners. The English legal system was complicated and intricate, and King William postponed any attempt to revise it.

The real changes came in the system of land ownership.

These changes came about because of the breakdown of the English nobility after the revolts of 1069 and 1070. Before those years, we see Edwin, Morcar, Waltheof, and Stigand joining in William's councils with such important Normans as Odo of Bayeux, William Fitz-Osbern, and Robert of Mortain. Several of Edward the Confessor's household officers retained their old posts. King Edward's sheriffs in Wiltshire, Somerset, and Warwickshire are known to have stayed in office. In 1069 more than two-thirds of England was governed by William through earls of English birth.

But the rebellions that followed altered that picture. By the end of William's reign hardly any Englishmen held high rank in their own country, and there were no English earls at all. A foreign-born aristocracy had come to take complete command of the conquered nation.

The foreigners brought with them the feudal system. In this typically medieval social arrangement it was considered that all land was owned by the king. He then granted it to a small group of important barons, who in return promised to render military service to their ruler. The barons subdivided part of their land to lesser knights, also in return for an oath of allegiance. The knights, in turn, rented land to peasants, who paid for it with produce and manual labor. Society took the form of a great pyramid, with the king at the top, barons, knights, and peasants beneath him, and a great mass of serfs, or slaves, at the very bottom.

The king was the *liege*, from an old Germanic word meaning "free." Those who swore fealty to him were *liege men*, or *vassals*. A feudal grant of land from liege to vassal was called a *fief*. The grant was made in a formal ceremony. The vassal knelt bareheaded before his lord and declared, "Hear, my lord, I become liege man of yours for life and limb and earthly regard, and I will keep faith and loyalty to you for life and death, God help me."

The feudal system was not a Norman invention. But under the Normans it became a highly complex and powerful social structure, typical of the system that dominated western Europe for the next several hundred years, until the rise of cities and powerful middle-class merchants fatally crippled the old king-baron-knight-peasant relationship.

England before the Norman Conquest had not attained a true feudal system. Like every other country in Europe, England had been approaching feudalism. But it took the Normans to establish the system in its true character.

In Anglo-Saxon England the king owned a great deal of the land, but by no means all of it. Much of the land originally was owned by free men, acknowledging no lord except the king. As the centuries passed, power and property began to concentrate in the hands of a few men. An informal feudal system developed, in which small knights or peasants might "commend" themselves to a great lord, transfer their land to him, and become tenants of his in return for his protection.

But this was not real feudalism because there was no rising pyramid of obligations. Any time the peasant or small knight grew dissatisfied with the protection he was receiving from his lord, he could dissolve the arrangement and commend himself to some other lord. And the powerful lords themselves owed no obligation to the king. Every man in the kingdom had a fierce measure of personal independence.

Under such a system, a great earl like Godwin could set himself up virtually as a king within the kingdom, ruling supreme over his own territory. And, under such a system, the king could not count on military service from his people, because they were not bound to him by feudal oaths. Duke William could command an army simply by summoning it. King Harold could not, and, as we have seen, was forced to disband his army, despite the Norman threat, because the bonds that held it were not strong enough.

England had had a complicated history, and so its pattern of society before the Conquest is not easy to describe. We find different laws and customs in different districts. Each of the old kingdoms of Mercia, Wessex, East Anglia, Northumbria, and the others had its own social structure, and the invading Danes who settled in the Danelaw brought customs of their own. So we cannot talk about the way of life in Anglo-Saxon England as though it were the same in every part of the land.

But we can try to simplify without oversimplifying. At the top of the Anglo-Saxon structure was the king. As we have seen, his powers were limited, and his grasp of the throne itself was sometimes shaky. The king owned great tracts of land, which he frequently presented to important nobles or churchmen to hold their loyalty.

A step below the king came the great nobles—originally called *ealdormen*, later *earls*. They varied in number, depending on shifting political alignments in England. In the time of Edward the Confessor there were only three great earldoms, those of Wessex, Mercia, and Northumbria, and the three earls were almost as powerful as the king. One of William's acts was to break up these big earldoms and create a great many smaller ones, to prevent such a concentration of power.

The earls were landlords. They owned whole counties, inhabited by thousands of farmers, who paid rent of various kinds for the right to live on the earl's property. There were also smaller landowners, a lesser nobility. These were the *thegns*. The word originally meant "one who serves another" and applied to the companions of the monarch. The leading thegns served at court and filled high offices in the kingdom. Each earl was also surrounded by a cluster of thegns, aiding him in the task of governing the earldom and receiving land from him in return. Then there were smaller thegns, who owned little land and who were bound by oath to serve the king or an earl or even a greater thegn. Even the poorest thegn, though, considered himself a man of high birth.

Below thegnly rank came the peasants. There were many

different classes of small farmers. Some—particularly in the Danelaw—owned their land outright and were free of all rent to noblemen. Others were tenants, and still others were little more than slaves. We cannot begin to discuss these different classes in detail.

One document, though, gives us an idea of the social structure as it existed in at least one part of pre-Conquest England. This is a treatise on estate management called the *Rectitudines Singularum Personarum,* written in the time of King Edward the Confessor.

This work divides the peasantry into three classes. First comes the *geneatas,* a kind of peasant aristocracy. A *geneat* paid his lord annual rent in farm produce and gave him a swine a year for pasture rights. He was expected to keep guard on the lord's property, to help in the reaping of his harvest, to help maintain the hedges around the lord's house. Otherwise he was free to farm his own land for his own benefit.

A notch downward came the *kotsetla.* He, too, paid rent in the form of services. On some estates he was required to give his lord service in the fields every Monday in the year, and on three days a week in August. A day's work consisted of reaping an acre of oats and half an acre of other grain. When ordered he had to perform other small services for the lord.

The bulk of the peasants were called *geburas.* They were required to work for the lord two days a week all year, three days a week in springtime and again at harvest time. Beside this, they were obliged to plough an acre a week in the fall, to guard the lord's flocks in winter, and to pay as rent each year ten pence in cash, twenty-three bushels of barley, two hens, and a young sheep. Each *gebur* was entitled to receive from his lord when starting out two oxen, a cow, six sheep, seven acres of land, farming tools, and furniture for his house. When a gebur died, the lord took possession of all his property.

All these various classes of peasants were known by the general term *ceorl*, which simply meant a member of the lowest class of freemen. The word is still in our language today, as "churl," but it has come to mean "a rude low-bred fellow, one who is stubborn, grudging, brutal, surly, uncooperative." Below the ceorls were the slaves—captives taken in war, or members of the race of Britons who had been shoved aside by the invading Angles and Saxons in the fifth and sixth centuries. Slaves did not play an important role in English life.

The English system that William found was loose and informal. The germs of feudalism were there—especially in the powerful earldoms developed fifty years before the Conquest. But everything was too uncertain, too vaguely organized. There was no real backbone to the English system.

King William gave it one. He swept away the old arrangement whereby a ceorl or lesser thegn chose the lord he wished to commend himself to. No longer could a man who owned a small plot of land change masters at will. The small English landlord was wiped out. He had to surrender his land—and then it was given back to him as a feudal fief.

A new Norman aristocracy took over the earldoms. Norman barons replaced the major thegns. All land was held in fief from the king and subdivided down to the peasantry. The distinctions among *geneat, kotsetla, gebur,* and the other kinds of freeman were wiped out. They were all lumped together under the Norman term of *villein*, which simply meant one who holds his land as a feudal tenant and not to be confused with "villain." There were no longer any freemen. Everyone in England held his land either as a tenant of the king or as a tenant of some lord who himself held his land as a fief from the king.

Most important, every feudal vassal in England had to swear allegiance, not only to his lord, but to the man at the top of the pyramid—the king. William was the supreme lord. In Anglo-Saxon England it was possible for a man to owe allegiance, say, to Earl Godwin, but not to King Edward. Now, in the case of any conflict between a king and a baron, the vassals were obliged to support the king, regardless of any oaths they might have sworn to a rebellious baron. This spared King William some of the problems of feudal rulers in other parts of Europe, such as the King of France or the Emperor in Germany. Those rulers were plagued with vassals who regarded themselves as petty kings in their own fiefs, made private war on their neighbors, and paid little heed to the words of the liege lord. William himself, as Duke of Normandy, was a vassal of the King of France, but never troubled himself overmuch to do feudal homage. He took good care that none of *his* vassals would have the same degree of independence.

The reorganization of England was largely carried out in a decade, from 1070 to 1080. England was transformed into a feudal state. The weaknesses that had hampered England for hundreds of years were eliminated. In one swoop William cleared away the debris of the various Old-English kingdoms, creating new subdivisions that cut across the lines of the old ones. He put Normans in charge and reduced the English to secondary rank. And he placed himself firmly and unshakeably at the top of the whole system.

WILLIAM'S LATER YEARS were troubled ones. Although he had subdued the English and ended the threat of an uprising by the conquered people, he still had enemies to deal with.

One of them was his own eldest son Robert, nicknamed Curthose because of his short legs. A powerfully built, lively young man, Robert enjoyed the better things of life and spent money freely to keep himself and his gay companions amused.

Robert's chief flaw was an overeagerness to succeed his father. When William had completed his conquest of England, Robert approached him with a suggestion that the duke turn over Normandy to him. William had all England to rule; why did he need to keep his title in Normandy as well?

The suggestion infuriated William. "It is not my custom to take off my clothes before I go to bed," he retorted angrily. Father and son quarreled. William refused to yield power to him, and finally Robert went abroad, wandering from land to land. His mother, Queen Matilda, secretly sent money to him, and this angered William all the more.

Robert eventually ran short of money. He turned to his cousin, King Philip of France, for aid. Philip and Robert decided to invade Normandy and overthrow William. It was agreed that Robert would be duke, but that Philip and his Frenchmen would be liberally paid for their part in the plot. This was in 1078.

William was in Rouen when word reached him of his son's treachery. He led an army against Robert, who had taken possession of the castle of Gerberoy on the Norman border. For three weeks an army of English and Norman soldiers besieged the castle, but Robert held out. One story says that father and son did hand-to-hand battle against one another, without knowing who it was they fought, and that William was actually wounded by his son, and might have been slain but for the aid of an English knight named Tokig of Wallingford.

William was unable to take the castle. It was the first real military defeat the aging Conqueror had ever suffered. Some saw in it an omen for the future. Finally he came to terms with King Philip and withdrew from Gerberoy.

Some months later father and son were reconciled briefly. In 1080 there is record of King William's sending Robert toward Scotland to head off a possible invasion of Northumbria by King Malcolm. But soon William and Robert quarreled again, and Robert went into exile in France. William put a curse on him as he departed.

There were other family sorrows for the Conqueror. His second son, Richard, was killed in a hunting accident soon after Robert's final quarrel with his father. King William had ordered more than sixty villages destroyed to create what was called the New Forest, for the hunting pleasure of the Normans. Many an Englishman cursed the king when he had to surrender his farm and home to help form the New Forest, and many an Englishman quietly rejoiced when young Richard spurred his horse into a tree's overhanging branches, was thrust against the pommel of his saddle, and died.

Soon after, William's daughter Agatha died while journeying toward Spain, where she was to marry King Alfonso of Galicia. And then, in 1083, Queen Matilda herself died. William saw his family stealing away from him, one at a time, while he grew older and more bitter in his loneliness.

And there was trouble among William's own barons. Men of Brittany and men of Normandy conspired against the Conqueror in 1076, rising against him in revolt.

The conspiracy began with a marriage. Earl Roger of Hereford, the son of William Fitz-Osbern, had arranged to give his sister Emma in marriage to Ralph of Norfolk, son of Ralph the chamberlain, one of Edward the Confessor's ministers. For reasons which we do not know, King William sent orders forbidding the marriage. It was celebrated in defiance of the king.

A great wedding feast was held. Norman barons and bishops came by the dozens, along with Welsh chiefs invited by Ralph of Norfolk, and the one remaining great English lord, Waltheof, Earl of Huntingdon, Northampton, and Northumberland, and husband of the Conqueror's niece Judith.

The barons drank freely at the feast, and soon some of the more outspoken were muttering against William. They were weary of serving him, they said. And they longed to divide up the rich English lands which William had reserved for his own use after the Conquest. Roger of Hereford and Ralph of Norfolk led the conspiracy, and they invited Earl Waltheof to join them in rebellion against the king.

The rebels began to collect an army. But as Roger of Hereford started to march eastward he was met by a Norman force under loyal barons, and the aged English Bishop Wulfstan of Worcester ordered him to turn back. Archbishop Lanfranc of Canterbury also took a hand. Lanfranc excommunicated Roger because he had "renounced the faith which his father kept all his life towards his lords, and which gained him such great riches." William was in Normandy, and Lanfranc wrote to him there, telling him, "It were with great pleasure, and as a messenger from God Himself, that we should see you again among us. Do not hasten, however, to cross the sea, for it were shame on us were you obliged to come and assist us in destroying a handful of traitors and robbers."

William did not hurry back. The royal army, under Bishop Odo of Bayeux, Bishop Geoffrey of Coutances, and William of Warenne, moved against the rebels and defeated them quickly. Ralph of Norfolk's army was beaten at Fagadon, and every rebel lost his right foot as punishment. Ralph of Norfolk and his bride Emma made their escape and were banished from England forever, losing all their extensive lands. Earl Roger of Hereford was also smashed. He was taken prisoner and sentenced to captivity and the forfeiture of all his property. He was confined in the castle of Rouen.

Later William relented somewhat and sent his prisoner a rich wardrobe of clothing as an Easter gift. Roger showed his scorn for his captor by building a great fire in his cell and burning all that William had given him. When he heard the story, William flew into wrath. "It is a mark of pride and insolence," he blazed, "to affront me thus. By the splendor of God, this man shall not go out of his prison as long as I live!" Nor did he. Roger of Hereford remained in the castle of Rouen till the end of his days.

The most severe punishment of all fell upon the man who seems least to have merited harsh treatment. He was Earl Waltheof, the last great English lord. Although Ralph and Roger had invited him to join the conspiracy, he had never actually taken up arms against King William. He had broken with the plotters and had confessed to Lanfranc.

Waltheof had powerful Norman enemies. The barons hungrily eyed his lands and wondered why an Englishman should have remained so wealthy so long. They agitated for his execution. William was uneasy about executing

Waltheof, and for more than a year the earl languished in prison while the Normans debated his fate. Finally he was led forth, early on a May morning, to face the headsman's ax. Quietly Waltheof distributed his richly embroidered garments among the spectators, prayed, and presented himself for the deathblow. With the falling of the ax upon the neck of Waltheof, the Old-English earldoms were extinguished. Only one solitary royal figure remained, and that a shadowy one, the fugitive Edgar the Atheling. Edgar lurked at the court of his brother-in-law, King Malcolm of Scotland, and together they hatched plots against William that never came to fruition.

Waltheof's lands were divided. His earldom of Northumberland was given to Walcher, Bishop of Durham, whose reign ended with his murder in 1080, during another northern disturbance. The weary William quelled that uprising as he had done all the others, but his powers were slackening. From 1077 to 1080 he was absent from England entirely, busy with a long and difficult struggle to keep the French province of Maine from slipping from Normandy's grasp. His enemy now was Fulk, the new Count of Anjou, the strongest foe William had faced at home in decades. Fulk held William to a standstill, and the now elderly conqueror came to peace with him. Under an agreement in 1081, William's son Robert was allowed to have the title of Count of Maine, but Fulk of Anjou would be his feudal overlord.

Troubled in his home domain of Normandy, troubled by constant threats from Malcolm and Edgar in Scotland, troubled by unruly Welsh border chieftains, troubled by the ambitions of his own barons, King William knew no quiet in his declining years. Yet, for all the distractions that occupied him, he found time to rule, and to rule well. The Anglo-Saxon Chronicle for the year 1087 gives this description of King William:

> If any would know what manner of man King William was, the glory that he obtained, and of how many lands he was lord; then will we describe him as we have known him, we, who have looked upon him, and who once lived in his court. This King William, of whom we are speaking, was a very wise and a great man, and more honored and more powerful than any of his predecessors. He was mild to those good men who loved God, but severe beyond measure towards those who withstood his will. He founded a noble monastery on the spot where God permitted him to conquer England, and he established monks in it, and he made it very rich. In his days the great monastery at Canterbury was built, and many others also throughout England. . . .
> King William was also held in much reverence: he wore his crown three times every year when he was in England: at Easter he wore it at Winchester, at Pentecost at Westminster, and at Christmas at Gloucester. And at these times, all the men of England were with him, archbishops, bishops, abbots, and earls, thegns and knights.

The Chronicle tells of William's wrath against those who offended him. "He removed bishops from their sees, and abbots from their offices, and he imprisoned thegns." And, we learn, "at length he spared not his own brother Odo."

The quarrel with Odo was the most startling step William took in his later years. The warrior-bishop Odo had been William's right hand for more than twenty years. William had made Odo one of the wealthiest and most powerful earls in England. He was also one of the most hated men in England, for his cruelty and greed were legendary. After the Northumbrian troubles of 1080, William sent Odo to lay waste the north as William had done many years before, but Odo did it with such ferocity that William himself seems to have been shocked.

What touched off the quarrel between the brothers is uncertain. Perhaps Archbishop Lanfranc, who had never liked Odo, warned William that Odo was getting too powerful. Perhaps it was William's annoyance at Odo's increasing boastfulness. Possibly it was Odo's plans to travel to Italy with an entourage of Norman knights in the hopes of being elected pope. William was known to oppose this idea, because he needed the knights to defend England and was far from eager to see his brother ascend the papal throne.

In 1082, while Odo prepared to leave for Rome, William called his barons together. He recited a list of Odo's offenses against justice. "Consider these grievances," King William said, "and tell me how I should act to such a brother."

There was no answer. No one dared get involved in the dispute between the powerful brothers.

"Let him then," William ordered, "be arrested and placed in safe custody!"

Odo was present at the meeting. No one was bold enough to seize him. Finally William himself came forward to grab his brother firmly by the arm.

"I am a priest!" Odo cried. "I am the minister of the Lord. The Pope alone can judge me!"

William, always ready with a tricky legal argument, replied, "It is not the bishop or the priest whom I judge. It is the earl, my vassal and false viceroy, whom I arrest."

Odo was hurried to Normandy, and joined other distinguished prisoners in the castle at Rouen. Only on his deathbed, five years later, did William grudgingly release Odo. It proved to be a mistake. As soon as he was released he hurried to England, where he tried to lead a revolt against his nephew, the new king, William II. The revolt was crushed, and Odo fled to Normandy, where he lived for eight years. In old age he set out for Jerusalem, joining an army that had sworn to liberate the Holy Land from Moslem rule. A warrior to the end, Odo never fought in the Crusade. He died in Italy, less than halfway to Jerusalem, in 1097.

The chronicler tells us how King William maintained law and order in England.

> It was such that any man might travel over the kingdom with a bosomful of gold, unmolested; and no man dared kill another, however great the injury he might have received from him. . . . The land of the Welsh was under his sway, and he built castles therein; moreover he had full dominion over the Isle of Man; Scotland also was subject to him, from his great strength; the land of Normandy was his inheritance, and he possessed the earldom of Maine; and had he lived two years longer he would have subdued Ireland by his prowess, and that without a battle.

There was a darker side to William's reign, as the Chronicle notes:

> Truly there was much trouble in these times, and very great distress; he caused castles to be built, and

oppressed the poor. The king was also of great sternness, and he took from his subjects many marks of gold and many hundred pounds of silver, and this either with or without right, and with little need. He was given to avarice, and greedily loved gain.

Like Edward the Confessor before him, King William enjoyed the sport of hunting. "He made large forests for the deer, and enacted laws therewith, so that whoever killed a hart or a hind should be blinded. As he forbade killing the deer, so also the boars; and he loved the tall stags as if he were their father. He also appointed concerning the hares, that they should go free." All these game animals were reserved, of course, for William himself, and woe betide the man who poached on the royal preserves! "The rich complained and the poor murmured, but he was so sturdy that he recked nought of them; they must will all that the king willed, if they would live, or would keep their lands, or would hold their possessions, or would be maintained in their rights. . . ."

NEAR THE CLOSE OF WILLIAM'S REIGN the old threat of invasion from Denmark, which had menaced England for two hundred fifty years, was revived for the last time. King Sweyn Estrithson had died in 1076 and was succeeded by his son Harold. Harold in turn died in 1081, and to the Danish throne came his brother, who bore the historic name of Cnut.

Cnut had dreams of repeating the feat of the hero for whom he had been named, and making himself King of England. He revived his father's old claim to the English throne, and formed an alliance with King Olaf of Norway and Count Robert of Flanders. They formed a powerful navy, even stronger than that of Harold Hardrada. More than a thousand Danish ships were assembled, with hundreds more from Flanders, and sixty from Norway.

When this threat appeared, William was once again warring in the troublesome province of Maine. He was nearly sixty, and had grown enormously fat in later years, though his old strength and vigor had not left him. Quickly bringing an end to his conflict in Maine, William hired all the Norman, French, and Breton knights he could find and returned to England. So vast was the invading fleet that William decided it would be impossible to defend the eastern coast of England against it. He gave orders for all supplies which might be useful to an invader to be removed from the coast, and hoped to take his stand inland against the Danes.

The invasion never came. The Danish fleet mutinied against Cnut, the other allies pulled out, and finally, in 1086, Cnut was murdered by his own subjects. The Danish threat passed and never arose again.

The short-lived danger, though, awakened King William to a weakness of his administration. During the national emergency he had ordered a tax placed on all Englishmen, to support the war effort if the Danes attacked. It became evident that the government did not have a very clear idea of who owned what in England and so could not assess taxes properly.

So, late in 1085, William "held very deep speech with his council about this land—how it was peopled, and with what sort of men." It was decided to take a great survey of the entire land. A chronicler writing in 1086, Bishop Robert of Hereford, is our best authority for the nature of this survey.

Bishop Robert writes that, at King William's order,

> A description of all England was made this year in the fields of the various provinces, in the holdings of the various lords, in their fields, in houses, in men both bond and free, both in those living only in cottages and in those having houses and fields, in ploughs, in horses and other beasts, in the service and rent of the land of all. Some commissioners were sent after the others, and commissioners were sent into places where they were not known and which they did not know in order to check each other's reports and inform the king of those accused of error.

The commissioners asked many questions. They summoned the king's sheriffs, the barons of each shire, the parish priests, the reeves, or local justices of the peace, and ordinary villagers. All were placed under oath and asked to give information about the land in their possession in the time of King Edward, in the time when King William gave it to them, and today. No mention was made of the reign of King Harold, which William considered an unlawful reign.

According to Robert of Hereford, the commissioners in each village asked the name of the manor, "who held it in the time of King Edward, who holds it now; how many plough teams on the lord's land; how many men; how many villeins; how many cottage dwellers; how many slaves; how many freemen; how much woodland; how much meadow; how much pasture, how many mills; how many fish ponds."

So minute was the questioning that one English chronicler was able to say, "Being sharp-sighted to his own interest, King William surveyed the kingdom so thoroughly that there was not a single hide of land throughout the whole, of which he knew not the possessor, and how much it was worth, and this he afterwards entered in his register." And another chronicler sounds a trifle disturbed that so mighty a personage as the king should deign to ask such trifling questions: "So very narrowly he sought it out, that there was not a single hide nor yard of land, nor so much as—it is shameful to tell and he thought it no shame to do—an ox nor a cow nor a swine was left that was not set in his writ."

This enormous undertaking was carried out in less than a year. The farmers and small landholders of England were reluctant to cooperate with the king's commissioners, just as the same sort of people today take offense at the prying questions of tax agents and other "revenooers." But they cooperated, out of fear of William, though several commissioners lost their lives while carrying out their duties.

The information, on roll after roll of parchment inscribed in Latin, was sent to the royal treasury at Winchester. The record covered all of England except the four northern counties and a few towns, including London and Winchester. Why these towns were not included, we do not know. It is an unfortunate loss, since otherwise we would know much about the size of London in King William's day that we do not know today.

From the parchment rolls the clerks compiled The Book of Winchester, two ponderous volumes of statistics, nicknamed the Domesday Book by the English, as though the Day of Judgment had come and the property of all men was being recorded. Domesday Book still exists, treasured at the Records Office in London. It is unique in medieval history. No document can be compared to it. It is a superb record of England as it was in 1066 and 1086, and much that we know about English history we know only thanks to this amazing land-register that King William caused to be compiled. As the historian Sir Frank Stenton puts it, "As an administrative achievement it has no parallel in medieval history. It is a supreme demonstration of the efficiency of those who served the Conqueror, and of the energy with which at the end of his reign he could still enforce the execution of a great design."

ONLY ONE IMPORTANT PUBLIC ACT remained to William as King of England after Domesday Book. On August 1, 1086, the king called together at Salisbury "all the land-holding men of any account throughout England whosoever men they were." One chronicle says that 60,000 men were there.

King William confronted the nobility of England—the earls, the barons, and abbots, the knights and minor thegns. Solemnly he asked them to take a personal oath of fealty to him. It was an oath designed to transcend all other feudal claims. Now, at the close of his reign, William the Conqueror asked all the notables of England to swear to be faithful to the king at all times, to defend him against all his enemies, to support him against all other men.

They swore the oath. It was the final touch to William's feudal structure. Now all of England, for the first time, owed allegiance to the king. If they were present that day, the ghosts of the old Anglo-Saxon kings must have felt pangs of envy at William's supremacy. Not Alfred the Great nor Offa nor Ethelbald nor any of the other strong kings had ever remotely achieved any such power in England. This was a new idea for England.

At the end of 1086 William left England for the last

time. He was old, as age was viewed in those days, and stout and balding, his body plagued by many ills. His wife and some of his children were dead. His eldest son was living in banishment. For half a century William had defeated enemy after enemy, and the strain of a lifetime of warfare had told on him. He had grown harsh and greedy, and the noble generosity of his early days was rarely seen now. Men feared him, and with reason, for they saw how he had dealt with his own brother Odo. His companions of the great old days were dead, and he spent his days and nights in loneliness.

And even now there was no rest for him. War beckoned once again, calling him to the saddle.

The enemy now was King Philip of France. The dispute centered over a district called the Vexin, on the border between France and Normandy. Dukes of Normandy and kings of France had quarreled over the Vexin for centuries. Long before William's day, France and Normandy had divided the Vexin between them. But in the days of William's father, Duke Robert, the French King Henry had given the Normans supremacy over the French half of the Vexin as well.

In 1077 Henry's successor, Philip, took back the gift. For the next ten years Normans and French bickered over the territory. Then, in 1087, while William rested in his palace at Rouen and made a valiant attempt to diet away his bulging paunch, the French crossed the border and raided the Norman half of the Vexin.

William stormed at this effrontery. He demanded that the whole Vexin be given to Normandy. Philip refused, and mocked William's obesity in the bargain. William, goaded to the point of fury, quitted his bed to invade the Vexin.

Toward the end of July, 1087, he marched into the

Vexin and took the French border town of Mantes. He captured the town by surprise and ordered it put to the torch. Fires blazed in Mantes, and the French fled. William, still a majestic figure even in corpulent old age, rode triumphantly through the streets as the houses of Mantes went up in flames. It was a nightmarish scene, with the giant old warrior glaring fiercely into the fires while his men looted and destroyed.

Plans were hatching in William's mind. Mantes had fallen easily. He would continue onward to Paris and hurl King Philip from his throne. Why not? Perhaps he even let the resonant words of a new title thunder through his mind: "William, by the Grace of God, Duke of Normandy, King of England and France."

Why not? It was a magnificent dream, worthy of a king.

It was never to be. As William rode through burning Mantes, his stallion, struggling already beneath his vast bulk, trod on a bit of burning wood. The horse stumbled. William was thrown violently forward against the iron pommel of his saddle. Gasping, he was helped from his horse, relieved of his armor. The old king had suffered a severe internal injury.

It was the end of the war of conquest against France. The Normans withdrew, bearing William on a litter, and sorrowfully wended their way back to Rouen. The king's physicians gathered round, but there was nothing they could do. Grimly but uncomplainingly William bore the agony of his wound.

For six weeks he lingered in terrible pain. The noise of busy Rouen became too much for him to stand, and he asked to be moved to the abbey of St. Gervais, overlooking the town.

William knew that he was dying. Toward the end he

sent for the great men of Normandy. Few who had triumphed over Harold with him at Hastings lived to see William die. The faces of young men hovered over him. Not even his son Robert was there, nor his half-brother Odo; Robert was still wandering in foreign lands, victim of his father's displeasure, while Odo lay a prisoner in the tower of Rouen. William's other two surviving sons were present: William, whom men called Rufus because of his red face, and young Henry, who had been born on English soil.

With these men gathered about him, the dying Conqueror uttered his last will and testament.

He began by reviewing the sixty years of his life. He had, he said, been brought up from infancy to be a warrior, and he had done much harm, shed much blood. He hoped he would be forgiven. For fifty-two years he had ruled Normandy, as wisely as he knew how. For twenty-one of those years it had been given him to be King of England as well.

He ordered that much of the great treasure he had amassed be distributed among the churches and abbeys of his dominions. He gave particular care to the churches of Mantes, which had been burned at his orders on his last, ill-starred expedition. He ordered the release of many political prisoners.

Lastly, William came to the difficult matter of his sons' heritage.

Though he had quarreled for years with his son Robert, William could not bring himself to disinherit him. He reminded the barons that long ago, before the battle of Hastings, he had named Robert as heir to the title of Duke of Normandy. William would not go back on his word now. Robert would be duke. But, the Conqueror said, he foresaw misfortune for Normandy. Robert, duke-to-be, was

William wounded at Mantes

cruel and foolish. He had William's ruthlessness but lacked William's core of piety and justice. Nonetheless, Normandy was his.

And the throne of England, won at such great cost?

"As for the kingdom of England," William said, "I bequeath it to no one, for it was not bequeathed to me. I acquired it by force and at the cost of blood. I leave it in the hands of God—only wishing that my son William, who has been submissive to me in all things, may obtain it if he please God and prosper."

William's lands were thus divided, to the horror of the Norman barons at the deathbed. Normandy to one son, England to another—a decree that put asunder what had been joined with blood. Many of the barons had possessions on both sides of the Channel, and now would find themselves owing loyalty to two masters. It was an impossible situation. Yet it helped to bring about great change. Many of the barons chose to give up their lands in Normandy and serve only the King of England. As the bond between the two parts of William's domain was severed, the aristocracy of England gradually stopped thinking of itself as Norman, and began regarding itself as—English.

King William's third son, young Henry, looked on in dismay as the Conqueror uttered his legacy.

"And what do you give me?" Henry asked.

"I give you five thousand pounds in silver from my treasury," William answered

"But what shall I do with this money," Henry asked, "if I have no land of my own?"

William's reply was prophetic. "My son, be content with your lot and trust in the Lord. Wait patiently while your brothers precede you. Robert will have Normandy and William will have England. As for you, when the time comes you will have all the possessions that I have acquired, and you will surpass your brothers in wealth and power."

In the last days of his life, King William consented to release his half-brother Odo from prison. He sank swiftly after that. As he lay on his deathbed, he could look back over a long and active life. He had been a great warrior and and a great king. He had weathered every imaginable kind of adversity, and had forged an imposing empire. Though he had been cruel when the need for cruelty arose, he had been more than just by the easy standards of his time. Perhaps he felt a moment of regret for what he had done to the brave King Harold, but it was not a pang that could have troubled the dying Conqueror for long. Harold had died heroically, and what more could a man ask than that? Better to go down on a battlefield than to lie slowly dying of a jab in the belly! Harold had lost a kingdom, but William certainly felt he had greatly strengthened England. He had taken a wealthy but weak and divided land, and had built it into a nation that soon would be the most mighty in Europe.

On the morning of Thursday, September 9, 1087, King William awoke from sleep to hear the sound of the great bell tolling in the cathedral at Rouen. He turned to a watcher at the deathbed and asked why the bell rang.

"Lord, it rings for the hour of Prime in the church of Our Lady," came the answer

William nodded. He raised his eyes, lifted high his hands. He said with as much of his old strength as he could muster, "I commend myself to the holy Mary, Mother of God, that by her prayers she may reconcile me with her Son, Our Lord Jesus Christ."

With those words the Conqueror died. An English chronicler later that year wrote, "Alas! that any man should so exalt himself, and carry himself in his pride over all! May Almighty God show mercy to his soul, and grant him the forgiveness of his sins!"

EVEN BEFORE his father had died, William Rufus had crossed into England, carrying with him a letter from William to Archbishop Lanfranc designating him as the heir to the English throne. When word came of the Conqueror's passing, William Rufus headed for the royal treasury at Winchester and took possession of it. Then he moved on to London, where he was proclaimed king without opposition, and crowned at Westminster on September 26.

The reign of William II lasted thirteen years. It was a time of troubles for England. The new king was vain and cruel and indolent, and was plagued with rebellion after rebellion. His great ambition was to defeat his brother Robert, now Duke of Normandy, and once again join England and Normandy under one rule. Robert, on the other hand, claimed the English throne, denouncing William II as a usurper. Brother contended with brother. By 1095, William II had gained control of nearly all of Normandy. A year later Robert, now duke in name only, developed the itch to go crusading. He pawned his title to William for 10,000 marks of gold, and left for Jerusalem, taking Odo of Bayeux and Edgar the Atheling with him. He was still abroad in the summer of 1100, when William II, hunting in his father's New Forest, mysteriously was struck down by an arrow and died, lamented by few.

The time of young Henry had come, as old King William had prophesied. Moving with his father's determination and vigor, Henry took the throne upon his brother's death. As Henry I he was a fit wearer of the Conqueror's crown, one of England's strongest and greatest kings. Six years after becoming king, Henry I met his elder brother Robert in battle, defeated him, and made him prisoner. Normandy returned to the hands of the English king; Duke Robert spent the last twenty-eight years of his life as his brother's captive. Normandy remained English for nearly a century, until it won its independence from weak King John in 1204, and the two lands went their separate ways.

As he lay on his deathbed, William the Conqueror could not have foreseen one strange irony. English blood returned to the English throne. His son Henry took as wife Edith, whom the Normans called Matilda, who was the niece of Edgar the Atheling, and a descendant of Alfred the Great and Cerdic of the remote past. The match won the hearts of Henry's English subjects.

Two children were born of that marriage: a prince named William, who died before his father, and a princess named Matilda. Henry's daughter Matilda married Geoffrey, Count of Anjou, who was descended from Geoffrey Martel, one of the Conqueror's bitterest enemies in the days when he was only Duke of Normandy. The son of Matilda and Geoffrey eventually came to the throne as Henry II.

It was an odd prank of fate. Only three full-blooded Norman kings ruled England: William I, William II, and Henry I. Those who came after mixed the blood of the Conqueror with that of the Counts of Anjou, and with that of the old Anglo-Saxon kings of Alfred's line.

Also marked with irony were the grotesque events immediately following the Conqueror's death. In the moment of William's passing, the barons and bishops gathered in Rouen fled the scene, hastening to their own homes even before the Conqueror's burial They feared that with the powerful ruler gone, anarchy and confusion would arise in Normandy, and they were eager to protect their own lands.

So William's body lay unguarded. Into the room where he reposed rushed servants, who made use of the opportunity to loot. They stole the king's furniture, even his bed, and his linens and clothing, and the gold and silver vessels from which he had eaten and drunk during his last illness. They left England's Conqueror lying nearly naked on the floor of the bare room in which he had died.

When the Archbishop of Rouen came to the abbey of St. Gervais, they found William thus. They set about transporting the king's body to Caen, where William wished to be buried at the abbey of St. Stephen. But no kinsman or servant of William could be found to prepare the body for burial.

The servants loot William's body

At last a knight of Rouen named Herluin stepped forward, "for the love of God and the honor of the people," to perform the last services for his master. He had the dead king embalmed and sewn up in an ox-hide, according to tradition, and accompanied it to Caen.

Priests and nobles waited there. The Conqueror's son William Rufus was off in England being crowned, but Henry was there, and Bishop Odo, newly released from prison, and many others to do homage for the last time to William the Conqueror. The funeral procession wound its way through the city, its destination the handsome abbey that William had built.

Fire had lent confusion to William's coronation in 1066. Fire accompanied him now. A blaze burst out in one of the wooden houses of Caen, and in moments spread from building to building in the tinder-dry town. The mourners fled, and only the monks of the abbey remained to carry William toward his last place of rest.

The fire was subdued, and the notables gathered again in the abbey church. Gilbert, Bishop of Evreux, preached the funeral sermon. When he had extolled William for his courage and greatness, he asked all present to pray for the soul of the departed king and to forgive him for any wrong he may have done them.

There was a sudden rude interruption. A man calling himself Ascelin, son of Arthur, shouldered his way to the front of the crowd and, in a voice that all might hear, cried, "This ground on which you stand was the site of my father's house. This man for whom you pray, while still only Duke of Normandy, took it away from my father by violence and built this church on it. I demand this ground and claim it publicly. In God's name, I forbid that the body of the robber should be covered with my earth and buried within my heritage!"

The ceremony halted. The Norman notables stared at one another in confusion. They conferred with men of Caen, soon learning the truth of Ascelin's charge. After a hasty discussion it was agreed to give Ascelin sixty shillings on the spot, and the king's son Henry promised to pay him a hundred pounds later on as compensation for the loss of his land. Only when this business was transacted could the funeral continue.

"All marveled," wrote Wace the chronicler, "that this great king, who had conquered so much and won so many cities and so many fine castles, could not call so much land his own as his body might lie in after his death."

IX

"WHAT IF—?"

Suppose William had lost at Hastings? What if there had been no Norman Conquest of England?

Let's try to play a favorite game of historians, the game of "What if—?" Let's try to imagine the course history might have taken, if only Harold had kept his throne that October day in 1066.

It could so easily have happened that way. The year 1066 is studded with crucial points where only a slight alteration of events could have sent William to defeat.

Consider:

Suppose William had sailed for England as originally planned, in August. He would have found Harold waiting with a skilled fleet and a fully equipped army. Very likely William's invasion force would have been hurled back in the Channel, and the would-be Conqueror himself sent to a watery grave. Even if he had managed to land on English shores, William would have had to face a grim and capable English army, determined to defend its homeland.

Suppose William had succeeded in making his Channel crossing early in September, instead of being turned back then by bad weather. Harold could quickly have reassembled his just-disbanded army. William would have landed safely, but he would have had a bitter struggle on his hands.

Suppose Harold Hardrada had not invaded England in the middle of September. Harold of England would then have had a fully rested army to throw against William, instead of a tired and weakened one. And the army of Earls Edwin and Morcar, which suffered so heavily at the hands of the Norwegians, would have been available to aid Harold against the invaders

Suppose Harold had been more patient in early October, when William actually landed. If instead of attacking right away, with a weary and only half-assembled army, Harold had waited and tried to starve William out, he probably would have succeeded. Winter was coming on. Once the snows of November and December began to fall, the Normans encamped in southeast England would have had a hard time supplying themselves with food. Cut off at sea by Harold's fleet, cut off on land by a solid line of English defenders, the Normans might have perished before the coming of the new year.

Suppose Harold had not been slain at Hastings. If he had lived to advise his men, they would perhaps not have been deceived by William's feigned retreats. The shield-wall would have held, and eventually the Normans would have had to fall back. In another few days reinforcements could have come to Harold's aid, and the tide would have turned forever against William.

There are five possible places in the span of two months where William might easily have gone down to defeat—if things had been otherwise. As we have seen, William's luck was remarkably good, and events conspired to place him on England's throne. But what if they had not? Can we reconstruct what might have happened if Harold had lived?

We can try.

Let's say that Harold still was King of England at the end of 1066, and that William was dead. Normandy certainly would have been divided among the enemies of William, such as the Count of Anjou and the King of France. William's oldest son, Robert, was still a boy, and not a very capable boy at that. He could never have held the dukedom the way his father, in a similar position thirty years before, had managed to do.

Harold, on the other hand, would be unchallenged in England—for a while. But in 1066 he had no legitimate sons, and he was past forty. Even assuming sons were born to him and Aldgyth in the years that followed, they might still have been children when Harold died. In the eleventh century few men lived to be as old as sixty. Harold might well have died a natural death by the year 1075, leaving behind a child of five or six as his only rightful heir.

There would have been another scramble for the English throne. Perhaps Edgar the Atheling, by then well into his twenties, would have come at last to the crown of his ancestors. Perhaps Edwin or Morcar would have usurped the throne. Or maybe King Sweyn of Denmark would have invaded successfully.

Whatever happened, England would be weakened and divided. Even if the crown remained in the family of Harold, the land would never become the unified nation William made it. Under the Anglo-Saxon system the individual earls had too much power. Edwin and Morcar would have remained constant threats to the king, either together or individually.

A seesaw would have resulted. Just as in the past, England would have been split between south and north. For a while the House of Wessex would have the upper hand, and then for a while the House of Northumbria or the House of Mercia. There would be no real unity, no national spirit. The death of each king would be a signal for an all-out civil war among the rival factions. Eventually England would be worn down into weakness and fatigue.

Meanwhile, across the Channel, a powerful enemy would be gaining strength. Perhaps he would be the King of France, perhaps the Count of Anjou. Quite possibly these titles would belong to one and the same man. If the ruling family of Anjou had gobbled up Normandy after William's "death" in 1066 and then had turned against young King Philip of France, much of what is France today would have been united under one leader. It would only be natural for him to look across the English Channel and dream of conquest.

And so, perhaps about the year 1150, an invasion fleet would gather in the ports of Normandy. Hundreds of French ships would sail for England, carrying warriors of Brittany and Normandy, of Maine and Anjou, of Paris and Aquitaine. The divided, weary Englishmen would be no match for the invaders. The English king—Harold IV, maybe, or Morcar II—would die on the battlefield or flee into exile. A French invader of the House of Anjou would then occupy the English throne.

Which is exactly what happened anyway in the real

course of history. Our investigation of the world of If has led us down a blind alley. It would seem that England was bound to fall, no matter what became of William in 1066. The build-in weaknesses and instabilities of the Anglo-Saxon kingdom seemed to guarantee that, come what may, a foreigner would hold the throne within a century after the death of Edward the Confessor—and a French-born foreigner at that.

Let's try a different time track. Let's try to picture an England that did *not* fall.

In this world of If, King Harold lived to a ripe old age. He understood England's problems, and once he had disposed of the double threats of William of Normandy and Harold of Norway, he set about remedying the situation.

His biggest problem was in the north, where Earls Edwin and Morcar held themselves almost independent. We can imagine the northern earls growing more troublesome year by year, until by about 1070 Harold feels it necessary to take arms against them. In a great battle near York, both Edwin and Morcar are slain. Harold gives the earldoms of the north to his brothers Gyrth and Leofwine. The House of Wessex is supreme in England. Harold's only possible opponent is Edgar the Atheling, but Harold wins him over, giving him the hand of his young daughter.

For the rest of his reign King Harold works diligently to strengthen England. He breaks down the power of the earls, makes the king supreme. When he dies, in 1085, he is universally beloved by all his people, and England is strong and prosperous. His eighteen-year-old son, who was not even born in 1066, takes the throne as Harold II, and his uncles, the earls of England, swear allegiance to him.

The centuries pass, and England remains strong and

united under the rule of the House of Wessex. Across the Channel in continental Europe there is turbulence and confusion, but the English take no part in it. It has long been the Anglo-Saxon tradition to stay out of European politics. Let the King of France and the Emperor of Germany and the Pope of Rome bicker and quarrel; England will have none of it!

The English remain isolationist. They live on an island, and their national character is shaped by that fact. They have little to do with the European mainland. The great powers of Europe are France and Germany, and they contend for supremacy during the Middle Ages.

In 1492 a Genoese adventurer named Columbus discovers what he thinks is India, but which other men realize is a new continent across the Atlantic The magnet of America draws explorers from many lands The Spanish and the Portuguese are first to stake their claims in the New World, but not long after the French and the Dutch also have their colonies there.

Not the English. Not in this time-track. In the sixteenth century of our imaginary world King Godwin IX is on the English throne, and he has no interest in sailing across the sea to found colonies in America. Let the French and Spanish have America! England is quite content as she is!

And so, while England slumbers in blissful isolation, more adventurous nations carve up the world. Portugal and the Netherlands fall by the wayside, and France and Spain emerge as the great colonial powers. Most of North America is settled by Frenchmen; Spain takes the rich land of South and Central America for her own. Later, Africa is opened up, and the French and Germans take possession of the lands of the black people.

By the twentieth century England is a very minor nation, so unimportant that no one bothers to invade her. The great powers of Europe are France and Germany, who meet again and again in bloody, destructive war. Across the Atlantic the one-time Spanish colonies have freed themselves from the tyrannical rule of the home country, and have become many independent republics. The southwest part of North America, from Texas to California, is broken up into a dozen Spanish-speaking republics. The rest of North America is one huge French-speaking commonwealth, stretching from the Atlantic to the Pacific, from the Gulf of Mexico to the Arctic Circle. It includes Alaska, which was purchased from the Czar of Russia in the 1860's. This great North American commonwealth pays its respects to the King of France, but is really independent in every way that counts, as Canada is in the world of our time-line.

England is insignificant. England never bothered to develop an overseas empire. England is a tenth-rate nation, left far behind in the modern world. But England has had peace for a thousand years, and the English king can trace his lineage back fifteen centuries to Cerdic.

So MUCH FOR FANTASY. In the real world, *our* world, William came and William conquered.

What were the effects of the Conquest, other than a mere change of ruler?

They were many and widespread. England became a unified land. The old Anglo-Saxon aristocracy was thrust into obscurity, and swaggering Normans came to rule. A new spirit was infused into England, a Viking spirit of boldness and adventure. From Normandy flocked not only aristocrats but merchants and artisans as well, bringing with them fresh blood, new ideas. Old Anglo-Saxon England had been stagnating, but the thousands of newcomers brought fresh vigor to an island reeling under decades of weakness and defeat.

Norman merchants and Norman artisans mingled with the English. New names appeared. A record of the town of Hastings taken soon after the Conquest showed a list of the new inhabitants, including "Gilbert the Foreigner, Gilbert the Weaver, Benet the Steward, Hugh the Secretary, Baldwin the Tailor." The Normans merged with the English on every level of society.

As they had absorbed the Danes in the ninth century, the English absorbed the Normans in the eleventh. For two centuries the Norman aristocracy spoke French while the common people spoke English, but gradually there came a blending of the races and of the languages The English language—with a heavy tinge of French, it is true—came to be the tongue of king as well as peasant. After the time of Henry II the nobility of England ceased referring to themselves as "Normans." They were simply Englishmen now, the sons and grandsons of men born on English soil. Henry II's wife was of the blood of Alfred, after all, and his royal sons Richard and John were thus half-English by birth. There were many other marriages between conquerors and conquered. The two races blended so rapidly into one that a new breed emerged by the thirteenth century. Out of the Anglo-Norman fusion came the medieval Englishmen.

They embodied the best attributes of both strains. From the Anglo-Saxon descent came an understanding and a respect of law and scholarship, an awareness of history and tradition. From the Norman line came strength, unity, the old Viking love of adventure. To quote the historian Frank Stenton: "The Normans who entered into the English inheritance were a harsh and violent race. They were the closest of all western peoples to the barbarian strain in the continental order. They had produced little in art or learning, and nothing in literature, that could be set beside the work of Englishmen. But politically, they were the masters of their world."

Out of the union of Norman and Saxon came the English kingdom that dominated Europe for centuries afterward, the strong England of Edward I and Henry V. Out of their union came the wealthy England whose goods were in demand all over Europe, whose merchants ventured far and wide. Out of that union came the England of Queen Elizabeth I, when bold descendants of Normans and Saxons crossed the Atlantic to found the colonies out of which the United States of America grew. Had there been no William the Conqueror, there would have been no great England in the centuries after him, and no great United States today.

Out of the union of Norman and Saxon, too, there came the English language we speak today, the language ennobled by Chaucer and Spenser and Shakespeare. It is a language very much different from that spoken by Edward the Confessor. The old Anglo-Saxon language was a Germanic tongue, heavily weighted by complicated grammatical forms. For centuries after the Conquest, English was spoken only by peasants, and during those years it lost its clumsy inflections and elaborate genders, and became the simple flexible language we use today.

And a strain of Norman French entered English to stay. Had there been no Norman Conquest, English vocabulary would be vastly different today. The Normans introduced thousands of words relating to hunting, war, politics, justice, religion, cooking, and art. Words like *baron, servant, messenger, feast, story,* and *noble* are part of our Norman heritage. So, too, are *roast, toast, boil, fry, soup, beef, veal,* and *pork*. And *vein, nerve, stomach, artery, tendon.*

Though many Norman words entered English, many thousands of good Anglo-Saxon words remained: *arm, hand, finger; harp* and *fiddles; shoe, glove,* and *smock; fire* and *cheese, father* and *foot, friend* and *foe.*

The most eloquent symbol of the blending of the races is shown by the wealth of synonyms English has today. Both the Norman and the Anglo-Saxon streams still flow freely in our language. We have *perceive* and *know, power* and *might, pray* and *beseech.* We have *cure* and *heal, foreword* and *preface, country* and *land,* and many another pair of synonyms. This double stream of words gives English a richness, a flexibility, a wealth of color, that no other European language can equal. The languages of Europe fall into two great families, the Romance languages such as French, Italian, and Spanish, derived from Latin, and the Teutonic languages, such as Swedish, German, and Dutch. Only English blends the Romance and the Teutonic, taking the best from both. Perhaps the English language of today was William the Conqueror's greatest gift to those who followed after him.

"This was a fatal day to England, a melancholy havoc of our dear country," wrote William of Malmesbury in 1120, speaking of the battle of Hastings.

The long view of history tells us otherwise. We can only feel sorrow for the tragic King Harold, a victim of the violent year 1066. But the day that saw old England die brought forth a new nation of glorious destiny. Out of the bloodshed of 1066 rises the massive figure of William the Conqueror. Of him, one of his biographers has written, "There was greatness in all he aimed at, all he achieved. There was greatness even in his failures, even in his crimes."

1066 was a year of decision. Looking back across nine centuries, we see blond Harold and black-haired William confronting one another on the field at Hastings. From the downfall of one, from the triumph of the other, came England in all her greatness, the land whom her greatest poet called

> This royal throne of kings, this scepter'd isle,
> This earth of majesty, this seat of Mars,
> This other Eden, demi-paradise;
> This fortress built by Nature for herself
> Against infection and the hand of war;
> This happy breed of men, this little world. . . .
> This blessed plot, this earth, this realm, this England.

BIBLIOGRAPHY

Cambridge Medieval History, Vol. V. Cambridge, England, Cambridge University Press, 1926.

Churchill, Sir Winston, *The Birth of Britain*. New York, Dodd, Mead, and Co., 1926.

Classen, E., and Harmer, F. E., eds., *The Anglo-Saxon Chronicle*. Manchester, England, Manchester University Press, 1926.

Creasy, Sir Edward, *The Fifteen Decisive Battles of the World*. London, Bentley and Son, 1851.

Du Chailu, Paul B., *The Viking Age*. New York, Charles Scribner's Sons, 1890.

Freeman, E. A., *History of the Norman Conquest*, Vols. I-VI. Oxford, England, Oxford University Press, 1867-1879.

Green, J. R., *A Short History of the English People*. London, 1888.

Hassall, W. O., ed., *They Saw It Happen*, Vol. I. Oxford, England, Basil Blackwell, Ltd., 1957.

Maclagan, Sir Eric, *The Bayeux Tapestry*. Harmondsworth, England, Penguin Books, Ltd., 1945.

Oman, Sir Charles, *England Before the Norman Conquest*. London, Methuen and Co., Ltd., 1910.

Pei, Mario, *The Story of English*. Philadelphia and New York, J. B. Lippincott Co., 1955.

Slocombe, George, *William the Conqueror*. New York, G. P. Putnam's Sons, 1959.

Stenton, D. M., *English Society in the Early Middle Ages*. Harmondsworth, England, Penguin Books, Ltd., 1952.

Stenton, Sir Frank, *Anglo-Saxon England*. Oxford, England, Oxford University Press, 1947.

Trevelyan, G. M., *History of England*, Vol. I, 3rd ed., revised. New York, Longmans, Green & Co., Inc., 1952.

INDEX

Alfred the Atheling, 23, 26, 27, 29, 30, 32, 43, 49, 78
Anglo-Saxons, 15, 18, 20, 21, 34, 167-171, 172

Churchill, Sir Winston, 17
Cnut (of Denmark), 181, 182
Cnut (of England), 23, 26-29, 30, 35, 36-37, 42, 43, 60, 78, 80, 143-144, 150, 156
Copsi, 72, 146, 154, 155
Cospatric, 69, 155, 157, 160

Danes, the, 5, 16, 21-30, 36, 80, 143, 144, 156-159, 160, 161, 163, 164, 168, 182
Denmark, 21, 27, 28, 60, 61, 68, 71, 72, 156, 163, 181
Dover, 32, 137-138, 148, 156

Edgar the Atheling, 154, 177, 192, 198, 200
    and William I, 141, 142, 147, 154, 155, 156, 157, 164, 165
    as claimant to throne, 4, 9, 40, 137, 139
Edmund Ironside, 9, 23, 26, 36
Edward the Confessor, 5, 27, 31, 37, 52, 60, 61, 63-64, 67, 111, 142, 146, 181
    and Godwin, 6-8, 32-33, 76
    and Harold, 38-39, 59
    and Tostig, 69, 70
    and William I, 7, 49, 56
    death of, 3-5, 10-12, 62, 111
    England under, 15-18, 33-34, 68
Edwin and Morcar, 67, 73, 74, 76, 136, 137, 140, 163, 164, 197, 198, 199, 200
    and Harold, 68, 69, 97
    and William I, 139, 141, 142, 144, 146, 147, 154, 156, 165, 166
    at Gate Fulford, 90-91, 110
Eldred, 12, 137, 141, 142, 143, 153
Ely, Isle of, 161, 162, 163

Emma, 10, 23, 26-27, 29, 31, 42
Estrith, 31, 43, 60, 71
Ethelred the Unready, 9, 16, 22-23, 26, 27, 29, 31, 42

Fitz-Osbern, William, 74, 80-81, 146, 148, 149, 156, 166, 174

Gate Fulford, 90, 91, 95, 97, 110
Geoffrey of Anjou, 46, 47, 48, 49, 80
Geoffrey of Coutances, 79, 117, 143, 176
Godwin, 7, 10, 17, 38, 49, 77, 78, 140, 150
    and Edward, 6, 31-33, 76
    family of, 35, 37, 38, 66, 67, 68, 69, 72
    rise to power, 29-30, 36-37
Gyrth, 67, 113-114, 127, 129, 133, 136, 200
Gytha, 43, 71, 135, 150, 152

Harold (of England), 35, 40, 77, 136, 137, 140, 142, 146, 147, 183, 190, 196-198, 200, 205-206
    and invasions, 70, 72, 73, 89-98, 107-130
    and William I, 50-59, 74-76, 78, 79, 82, 99, 141
    as claimant to throne, 4, 10, 11, 12
    as "under-king," 6, 7, 33, 38-39, 49, 66-69
    England under, 63-65
    military forces of, 83-86, 89, 92-93, 100-101, 102, 110, 117-118, 132-133
    succession to throne, 12-14
Harold Hardrada, 4, 10, 14, 18, 35, 39, 59-60, 61-62, 68, 97, 101, 102, 130, 136, 149, 182, 197, 200
    and Tostig, 71-72
    invasion of England by, 64, 87-96, 108, 112
Harold Harefoot, 29, 30, 144
Harthacnut, 5, 16, 27, 28-29, 30, 31, 32, 60
Hastings, 108, 109, 111, 112, 116-134, 136, 137, 144, 145, 148, 158, 188, 203
Henry I (of England), 153, 188, 190, 192-193, 194
Henry I (of France), 42, 45, 47, 186

Lanfranc, 74, 79, 161, 175, 176, 179, 191
Leofwine, 113, 129, 133, 136
London, 89, 92, 95, 98, 110, 111, 117, 136, 137, 139-140, 142, 144, 150, 184, 191

Magnus, 29, 30, 60, 61
Malcolm, 73, 88, 154, 164, 174, 177
Matilda, 50, 103, 148, 149, 153, 173, 174
Mercia, 11, 20, 66, 67, 68, 73, 139, 157, 168, 169
Morcar, see Edwin and Morcar

Normandy and the Normans, 4, 5, 6, 7, 23, 40-51, 54, 76, 163, 180, 188-189, 190, 192, 193, 197, 199, 202-203
    and Conquest of England, 80-85, 98-106, 107-109, 111, 112-113, 117-134, 137, 140-143, 157-158
    England under, 34, 144, 145, 165-172
    under William, 50, 51, 80, 147-149, 173, 174, 177, 186
Northumbria, 11, 20, 66, 68, 69, 70, 72, 73, 96, 139, 155, 157, 158, 168, 169, 174
Norway, 4, 27, 29, 40, 60, 68, 71, 73, 84, 87, 163, 182

Odo of Bayeux, 79, 81, 99, 117, 126, 146, 148, 149, 166, 176, 178-180, 188, 190, 192, 194

Philip I, 80, 173, 174, 186, 199
Popes, Roman Catholic, 50, 76-77, 78, 79

Riccall, 89, 90, 91, 92, 93, 96, 97
Robert (son of William I), 50, 149, 173, 174, 177, 188, 190, 192, 198
Robert, Archbishop, 5, 6, 7, 76, 78
Robert of Hereford, 182-183
Robert of Mortain, 48, 79, 81, 152, 166
Robert the Magnificent, 42-44, 45, 186

Scotland, 18, 20, 40, 88, 154, 164, 177, 180
Stamford Bridge, 91, 92, 93, 97, 107, 110, 117, 130
Stigand, Archbishop, 6, 10, 12, 77, 78, 137, 140, 141-142, 146, 147, 160-161, 166

Sweyn (of Denmark), 22, 23, 26, 27, 156
Sweyn Estrithson, 4, 31, 37, 60, 68, 71, 156, 161, 162, 181
Sweyn Godwinsson, 37-38, 40

Tostig, 6, 13, 39, 96, 97, 112
    as Earl of Northumbria, 66, 67, 68, 69-70
    attempts to overthrow Harold, 70-74, 88-90, 94-95

Wace, Robert, 99, 103, 104, 105, 108, 120-121, 122-123, 124, 125, 128, 129, 130-132, 134, 195
Wales, 18, 20, 38, 39, 160
Waltheof, 66, 146, 147, 149, 156, 157, 160, 166, 175, 176, 177
Wessex, 12, 18, 20, 21, 66, 67, 110, 150, 157, 168, 169
William of Malmesbury, 37, 42, 116, 129, 132, 205
William of Poitiers, 81, 100, 135, 137, 138, 141
William I (the Conqueror), 18, 35, 61, 64, 141-142, 173, 178-180, 196-200, 202, 205, 206
    and Conquest of England, 68, 76-83, 84, 85, 98-99, 100, 101-106, 107-134, 135-142
    and Edward, 5, 7, 49
    and Harold, 51-59, 74-76
    and Tostig, 70, 72
    as claimant to throne, 4, 8, 10, 13, 40
    as ruler of Normandy, 45-49, 50, 186-187
    birth and early life, 43, 44
    conspiracies against, 174-176, 177
    coronation of, 142-143
    death of, 187-191, 192, 193, 194-195
    England under, 143-164, 165-169, 171-172, 178, 180-185
    military forces, 51, 98-99, 101, 105
William II, 50, 180, 188, 190, 191-192, 193, 194

York, 67, 68, 69, 89, 90, 91, 92, 97, 98, 107, 109, 110, 154, 155, 157, 158, 160

www.ingramcontent.com/pod-product-compliance
Lightning Source LLC
Chambersburg PA
CBHW032109090426
42743CB00007B/287